Training Spatial Abilities

Training Spatial Abilities

A Workbook for Students of Architecture

Andri Gerber (Ed.)

Birkhäuser
Basel

Editor
Andri Gerber
Professor Urban History, ZHAW Winterthur

Printed with the financial support of the
School of Architecture, Design and Civil Engineering,
ZHAW Winterthur

Acquisitions Editor: David Marold, Birkhäuser Verlag, AT-Vienna
Content and Production Editor: Angelika Gaal, Birkhäuser Verlag, AT-Vienna
Translation: Lindsay Blair Howe, CH-Zurich
Copy editing: Anna Roos, CH-Berne
Layout and cover design: Sven Schrape, DE-Berlin
Lithography: Pixelstorm, AT-Vienna
Printing: BELTZ Bad Langensalza GmbH, DE-Bad Langensalza

Library of Congress Control Number: 2019955722

Bibliographic information published by the German National Library
The German National Library lists this publication in the Deutsche Nationalbibliografie;
detailed bibliographic data are available on the Internet at http://dnb.dnb.de.

ISBN 978-3-0356-2043-6

German Print-ISBN 978-3-0356-2210-2

© 2020 Birkhäuser Verlag GmbH, Basel
P.O. Box 44, 4009 Basel, Switzerland
Part of Walter de Gruyter GmbH, Berlin/Boston

9 8 7 6 5 4 3 2 1

www.birkhauser.com

CONTENTS

TEST MATERIAL   51

SPACE IN OUR MINDS—THE FUTURE NOW

The architect's task is to assemble the world over and over again. The content of their work is determined by social challenges such as the climate change crisis, conflicts of interest, consumption of resources, economic growth, housing shortages, social transformation, and the opposing demands of a wide range of actors: clients, politicians, administrations, landowners, users, visitors, investors, entrepreneurs, businesspeople. These are juxtaposed with cultural constraints such as roads, bodies of water, topographies, trades, advancements in architecture and technology; and experience and knowledge in relation to gravity, natural hazards, and material properties that have been shaped over many centuries. Finally, architects also draw inspiration from disciplinary discussions about what the ideal city and appropriate building should be.

No architecture or physical city can emerge based on this plethora of relationships alone. It requires a translation of the accumulated contents into physical space, and into spatial sequences that stand in diverse relationship to the spatial sequences that already exist. Such a translation is not possible without spatial imagination—the ability to see space with an "inner eye," and to move through it and change it.

The fact that spatial imagination allows us to imagine possible futures and draw plans for them is not new to the architectural discourse. But is spatial imagination more developed in architects than in other individuals? Does imagination change over the course of architectural education and training? And can this spatial imagination be further developed?

The research on which this book is based addresses these questions. While architects piece the world together, it is up to the sciences to take the world apart again, in order to derive knowledge from it. Due to these contradictory pursuits, architects depend on alliances with research scientists and scientific approaches to be able to engage with the core challenges of their discipline. Thus, the methodology of our colleagues from the Chair of Cognitive Science and from the Chair for Research on Learning and Instruction have made an essential contribution to examining the thinking of architects and providing them with insight into their processes. Conversely, the spatial knowledge of the architects involved in this project made it possible to develop new tests with research participants, in which it is now possible to investigate more specific spatial knowledge, behavioral patterns, and cognitive abilities.

I will hint at one significant insight we have gained from this project: architectural education changes one's ability to imagine space. Derived from the methodology and didactics of architecture, exercises can be conceived to train the capacity for spatial imagination—to the benefit of other disciplines, too.

In light of our research findings, one could attempt to test the spatial imagination of prospective architects and, depending on the results, advise them whether or not to study the subject. However, this would be misguided—because a lack of spatial imagination can be countered and trained by analog and virtual model making, drawing, and linguistic skill. For architecture, it is therefore paramount to have a fundamental interest in the interplay between space and society, and society and architecture, aiming to create a more sustainable future.

Prof. Dr. Stefan Kurath,
Architect and Urbanist, Institute Urban Landscape, ZHAW

DEFINING SPATIAL ABILITIES

WHAT IS SO SPATIAL ABOUT ARCHITECTURE?

Andri Gerber

"Architecture cannot be in our thoughts without space also being in them. Even when we are unable to describe it, or when we lack names to designate their specificity, the sole mention of a distance, a size, an interval, supposes the presence of an air belonging to architecture. This fact could well be understood as one of the fundamental paradoxes of this discipline, which keeps us busy: architecture is articulated air, not just air, but the order of such an ethereal volume with other similar yet different volumes. The articulation of air is its disciplinary destiny."
Mauricio Pezo, Sofia von Ellrichshausen, 2016[1]

The Ghosts that Haunt the Discipline

This book is based on a research project conducted from 2016 to 2019 by the Institute Urban Landscape at the ZHAW (Prof. Dr. Kurath), in collaboration with the Chair of Cognitive Science (Prof. Dr. Hölscher), and the Chair for Research on Learning and Instruction (Prof. Dr. Stern) at the ETH Zurich. Both this publication and the research project were born out of a sense of frustration on our inability to speak more precisely about space and, as such, about architecture. Architectural discourse is doomed to fuzziness because of the peculiar nature of this great discipline. Without a doubt, the blurred nature of both architecture and the words used to describe it is not just a flaw, but also one of its poetic qualities. Nevertheless, this hinders any deeper understanding of the discipline and its processes. Moreover, this condition has often been an all-to-easy retreat to avoid questioning the work of architects, and instead raising an opaque wall between architecture and the "rest of the world." In a classic structuralist manner, in what follows, we would like to disassemble the wall—or at least remove some of the bricks that comprise it—and then put them back in their original position. If we want to better understand architecture and its processes, this is where we must begin. Space, then, because of its ambiguity and importance, serves as the perfect starting point for our endeavor.

In the past, architecture has been discussed in many terms. One only needs to flip through the pages of the many recently published architectural anthologies: style, nature, monumentality, place, form, utopia, proportions, structure, or technique, to mention but a few. They isolate singular features, aiming to help us understand what architecture is and how it works. Many of these terms/concepts were introduced from fields other than architecture—in contrast, how many terms inherent to architecture have had this impact, except perhaps *cella*/cell or *grotto*/grotesque?—and opened up and tied architecture to a particular cultural zeitgeist and influence. Over the course of centuries, these terms evolved, changed, and returned with a new—or sometimes the same—meaning for the architectural discourse. They have become the very bones of the discipline, and that which allows us to speak of it. Among these, "space" plays a special role, as it was only recently introduced into the vocabulary of architecture, and is much more difficult to describe. Furthermore, there are many disciplines that work with concepts of space: philosophy, sociology, mathematics, physics, and many more. However, most of these definitions of space do not overlap, or when they do, it leads to misunderstandings. This is problematic for architects, who tend to blur the boundaries of these differences in their discourses. There are classic references to space from other disciplines that haunt architecture, and they are repeated over and over, from Martin Heidegger's (1889–1976) *Bauen, Wohnen, Denken* (1951) to Gaston Bachelard's (1884–1962) *Poétique de l'espace* (1957). These references can be found in the many architectural anthologies that have included "space," but only few truly architectural examples are discussed here, with Bernard Tschumi as the sole exception.[2] Yet there are indeed references that identified the problem early on, and established a more architectural perspective on this matter. This included German architects Herman Sörgel (1885–1952), Fritz Schumacher (1869–1947), and German art historian Albert Erich Brinckmann (1881–1958). One has only to read the introduction to Schumacher's book *Der Geist der Baukunst (The Ghost/Spirit of Architecture)* from 1938 to locate all the problems outlined above: "When an architect ventures into the seemingly incalculable territory of literary works that are summed up by the concept of *Kunstphilosophie* (philosophy of art), he will at first feel dizzy. He sees different ghosts crowding around him. Ghosts that often feud with each other, and yet claim whoever comes close to them for themselves. He will hear

---

1   Pezo, Mauricio, and Sofia von Ellrichshausen. *Spatial Structure.* Copenhagen: Architectural Publisher, 2016, p. 14.

2   Hensel, Michael, Achim Menges, and Christopher Hight. *Space Reader: Heterogeneous Space in Architecture.* Chichester: Wiley, 2009.

his own inner language, which will at first appear to be foreign. It is a language that tries to translate the sensuous, which is familiar to him, into something that is non-sensuous: into concepts. The purpose of this is a lofty one; it could perhaps be formulated as attempting to derive the world of concepts from the realm of experience, from which the former emerges."[3] Schumacher speaks of the ghosts that haunt those concerned with architecture, and their attempts to translate the sensuous into the conceptual. Architects too often fall prey to these ghosts and give up their architectonic "life," to slightly over-dramatize the metaphor. Architecture is a discipline prone to frequent mood swings, which are expressed not only in different architectural styles but also when translating between languages. The past is quickly forgotten, if not a source for stylistic inspiration. As such, the concept of space, although a recent "discovery," it has already undergone significant changes: (re-)discovered at the end of the nineteenth and early twentieth century, modernist architects associated the term with tradition, and thus, repudiated it. Interestingly, Postmodernism later agreed with this negative bias towards space, and it was only in the 1990s with the rise of the notion of "atmosphere"—quite independently in the work of German philosopher Gernot Böhme[4] and Swiss architect Peter Zumthor[5]—that spatial qualities were at stake in architectural discourse once again. The recent book on architectural space, published by Chilean architects Mauricio Pezo and Sofia von Ellrichshausen and quoted at the beginning of this chapter, shows how this subject is still considered relevant—by young, contemporary architects, too.

If architecture has often hidden behind this wall of fuzziness, science has made many attempts to breach it, yet often without a thorough understanding of what architecture really is. Yet a few projects have managed a deeper understanding of architecture and its processes, without missing the target or going off-topic. For example, the pioneering work of Vinod Goel or Ömer Akin is excellent in this context although its applicability to architecture at first appears limited.[6] Investigations by researchers such as Thora Thenbrink, Masaki Suwa, or Barbara Tversky into the relationships of language, architecture, and gestures, or by John Gero with his cognitive studies on design education, are very promising and might yield new perspectives on how we look at architecture, its processes, and the relationship between mind and language in architecture.[7] There

are many scholars working in this field, yet fruitful products of this research have remained scarce—or it has not been possible to translate it back into architecture, to no small extent because architects are not interested in empirical evidence, although many people may dispute this statement. A particularly fascinating experiment on the nature of creativity was conducted by Donald MacKinnon (1903–1987), director of the Institute of Personality Assessment and Research (IPAR), as reported by Pierluigi Serrano in his book on this project. Along with experiments on other professions, between 1958–1959, 124 architects were invited to participate in three-day studies. Although architects such as Ludwig Mies van der Rohe (1886–1969) and Walter Gropius (1883–1969) declined, other famous architects such as Louis Kahn (1901–1974), Philip Johnson (1906–2005), Eero Saarinen (1910–1961), and Richard Neutra (1892–1970) participated in this experiment. The architects were subdivided into three groups, according to their creativity—assessed by a board of experts and by the architects themselves—and were led through a series of tasks. There were multiple ways in which creativity was measured over the course of three days: intellect, perceptual and cognitive functions, measures of interest and values, personality inventories, originality, aesthetic sensitivity, and artistic reactiveness, determined by interviews and projective tests.[8] The tests included both established and new tests, such as the Mosaic Construction Test developed by a member of the group, Frank Barron (1922–2002), prior to running the study. This was probably the largest psychological investigation of architects ever undertaken and it resulted in many interesting insights into the nature of creativity—and at the same time, many of the participating architects reported gaining insight through the procedure. Unfortunately, the planned book about this test was never published by MacKinnon and his team.

Architects, too, have been seduced by the possibility of an empirical approach to their craft, yet these encounters remain flirtations, as in the case of Walter Gropius's essay "Design Topics," published in *Magazine of Art* in 1947 and then republished in 1955 in his book *Scope of Total Architecture*. Here, he describes the latest findings of optics and spatial perception, to find that they had long been discussed in many architectural and urban designs of the past. He underscores that, while architecture as art retains a very personal dimension, it should be possible to better understand the rules that govern perception: light, space, mass, form, and color. The goal is to avoid vague expressions such as "the atmosphere of a building" or "the coziness of a room."[9] The essay is accompanied by a series

3   Schumacher, Fritz. *Der Geist der Baukunst.* Stuttgart/Berlin: Deutsche Verlags-Anstalt, 1938, p. 9.
4   Böhme, Gernot. *Atmosphäre: Essays zur neuen Aesthetik.* Frankfurt am Main: Suhrkamp, 1995. Böhme, Gernot. *Architektur und Atmosphäre.* Munich: Fink, 2006.
5   Zumthor, Peter. *Atmosphären: architektonische Umgebungen: die Dinge um mich herum.* Basel: Birkhäuser Verlag, 2006.
6   Goel, Vinod. *Sketches of Thought.* Cambridge, MA: MIT Press, 1995. Akin, Ömer. *Psychology of Architectural Design.* London: Pion Limited, 1986.
7   Suwa, Masaki, and Barbara Tversky. "What do Architects and Students perceive in their design sketches? A protocol Analysis." In *Design Studies* 18, 385–403, 1997. Kan, Wai Tak, and John Gero. *Quantitative Methods for*

Studying Design Protocols. Dodrecht: Springer Netherlands, 2017.
8   Serrano, Pierluigi. *The Creative Architect. Inside the great Midcentury Personality Study.* New York: The Monacelli Press, 2016, pp. 101, 103.
9   Gropius, Walter. "Is There a Science of Design?" In Walter Gropius. *Scope of Total Architecture* [1955], 33. New York: Collier Books, 1962.

of images from experiments and their application to architecture through a series of diagrams.

In the 1960s, with the rise of cybernetics and computer technology, a specific interest for the methods of architecture was born and discussed in several conferences and publications; such as the *Conference on Design Methods* in 1962 (published 1963), *Design Methods in Architecture* in 1967 (published 1969), and *The Design Methods Group First International Conference* in 1968 (published 1970).[10] All three conferences were interdisciplinary, including both architects and scientists; one of the most important players in this was architect Christopher Alexander, with his attempts to bridge mathematics and architecture. He spoke at both the first and the second conference. This interest was affirmed by the rise of semiotics and structuralism, which also produced much (pseudo)scientific research into the "meaning" of architecture, such as the work of Geoffrey Broadbent, initiator of the third design methods conference.[11]

The Bologna Process in Europe was an important trigger for the renewed interest in such matters. Several conferences and publications were dedicated to the particular distinction between research *by* design versus research *on* design. This included some initiated by the European Association for Architectural Education (EAAE), such as the *Research by Design* conference in 2000,[12] the *Communicating (by) Design* conference in 2009,[13] the *Theory by Design* conference in 2012,[14] and the *Knowing (by) Designing* conference in 2013,[15] among many others.

Few examples stand out here, even if awkward titles such as the recent "Neuroarchitecture" suggest that this topic has become rather fashionable. First and foremost, this includes the work of Gabriela Goldschmidt on the relationship between sketching and reasoning—primarily that sketching helps unfold visual displays that were not previously in the mind of the designer, but only arose during the sketching process.[16] Another architect that made an important contribution to this line of thinking is Harry Mallgrave, who was first introduced to the English-speaking

FIG. 14

FIG. 16: Interior of Cathedral in Sienna

FIG. 15: Girl in bathing suit   FIG. 17: Phenomenon of irradiation

FIG. 18: St. John in Lateran, Rome

1 Walter Gropius, *Diagram*, 1955

world with his book *Empathy, Form and Space* (published with Eleftherios Ikonomou), which investigated the writings of several German art historians and scientists on space and perception. Later, he tied this knowledge to current discoveries in cognitive sciences and applied them to the history of architecture, resulting in very interesting insight into the cognitive development of architecture over the centuries.[17] A final important reference is the ongoing work of the Academy of Neuroscience for Architecture, which offers a wide range of subjects and teaching programs.[18]

Bridging architecture and empirical studies is thus both possible and necessary. Yet, there is always another danger lurking: that of taking any scientific evidence as a given, and constructing a rigid application thereof in architecture. Fascinating examples of this can be found in the writings of architects such as Hermann Maertens, or later on, Otto Schubert, who both developed rigid systems of viewing

10 Jones, J. Christopher, and D. G. Thornley (eds.). *Conference on Design Methods.* Oxford: Pergamon Press, 1963. Moore, Gary T. (ed.). *Emerging Methods in Environmental Design and Planning, Proceedings of the Design Methods Group.* Cambridge, MA: MIT Press, 1970. Broadbent, Geoffrey, and Anthony Ward (eds.). *Design methods in architecture.* London: Lund Humphries, 1969.
11 Broadbent, Geoffrey, Richard Bunt, and Charles Jencks (eds.). *Signs, Symbols, and Architecture.* Chicester: Wiley, 1980.
12 Faculty of Architecture, Delft University of Technology/EAAE, *Research by Design*, International Conference, November 1–3 2000 (Delft: DUP Science, 2001).
13 Verbeke, Johan, and Adam Jakimowicz (eds.). *Communicating (by) Design*, Brussels: Hogeschool voor Wetenschap & Kunst; Gent: School of Architecture Sint-Lucas; Göteborg: Chalmers University of Technology, 2009.
14 Faculty for Design Sciences. *Theory by Design: Architectural Research Made explicit in the Design Teaching Studio.* Antwerp: Artesis University College, 2012.
15 Verbeke, Johan, and Burak Pak (eds.). *Knowing (by) Designing.* Brussels: LUCA, Sint-Lucas School of Architecture, 2013.
16 Goldschmidt, Gabriela. "The Dialectics of Sketching." In *Creativity Research Journal* 4, No. 2, 123–143, 1991. Goldschmidt, Gabriela. *Linkography: Unfolding the Design Process.* Cambridge, MA: MIT Press, 2014.

17 Mallgrave, Harry Francis. *Architect's Brain, Neuroscience, Creativity, and Architecture.* Malden: Wiley-Blackwell, 2010. Mallgrave, Harry Francis. *Architecture and Embodiment. The Implications of the New Sciences and Humanities for Design.* Abingdon, Oxon: Routledge, 2013.
18 http://anfarch.org.

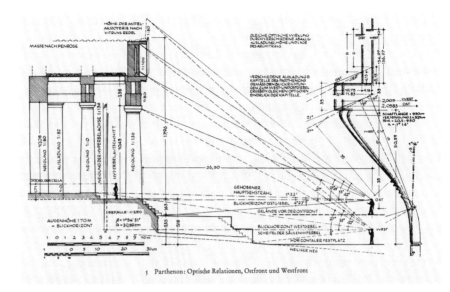

5 Parthenon: Optische Relationen, Ostfront und Westfront

angles out of findings in optics and perception. These were not only to be found in historical architecture, but should also be applied to the practice of design. In the words of Maertens: "The only purpose of a practical aesthetics of architecture, and the related arts that support it, should be to reveal the path to every practicing artist, primarily architects, of how to use theory to create aesthetic appeal for his fellow man in his work, which results from experience and research, even allowing him to strive for attaining perfect beauty."[19] The goal is thus to create a theory out of experience—yet, what resulted in this case were more rules and restrictions than an actual theory.

Spatial Ability Reloaded

As previously mentioned, the term "space" was introduced into the architectural discourse relatively late. It is of course obvious that architecture had been discussed in terms of inside and outside space, of perception and effect—yet not in terms of "space," (*Raum, espace,* or *spazio,* with each of the terms in their respective languages having quite a different depth and array of meaning). One must only peruse the literature by architects from every century to see how preoccupations with what we now understand as the term "space" have always been a central concern.

If we take, for example, a passage from *De re aedificatoria* (1485), by Leon Battista Alberti, everything is there—issues of perception and effect, tied to light, size, position, and relationship. He notes: "The greatest Commendation of the House itself is its making a cheerful Appearance to those that go a little Way out of Town to take the Air, as if it seemed to invite every Beholder: And for this Reason I would have it stand pretty high, but upon so easy an Ascent, that it should hardly be perceptible to those that go to it, till they find themselves at the Top, and a large Prospect opens itself to their View. (…). Lastly, what I have already said conduces extremely to the Pleasantness of all Buildings, I would have the Front and whole Body of the House perfectly well lighted, and that it be open to receive a great deal of Light and Sun, and a sufficient Quantity of wholesome Air. Let nothing be within View that can offend the Eye with a melancholy Shade."[20]

Space—intended as a matter of perception and expression of spatial configurations—has been a constant in architecture, mirrored by many insights that have emerged through the history of architecture, yet without ever establishing a unified theory. The closest architecture has come to such a theory is embodied by the heterogeneous group of physiologists, art historians, and architects who, at the turn of the nineteenth and early twentieth century, developed a true obsession with the matter of space. This development was described, as previously mentioned, by Harry Mallgrave, among others.[21]

Initiated during the Enlightenment and extended during Romanticism and by research into aesthetics in the seminal work by Alexander Gottlieb Baumgarten (1714–1762), grew an interweaving of opposite interests and directions of research, but united in the question of the origin and nature of sensations in their relation to thought, as exemplarily discussed by Immanuel Kant. In his *Critique of Pure Reason* (1781), Kant discussed space in relation to time extensively, but considered the former as something

19 Maertens, Hermann. *Skizze zu einer praktischen Ästhetik der Baukunst und der ihr dienenden Schwesternkünste.* Berlin: Verlag von Ernst Wasmuth, 1885, p. 5.

20 Alberti, Leon Battista. *Ten Books on Architecture,* Book IX, trans. James Leoni, London: Alec Tiranti, pp. 189-190.

21 I am only providing a short overview of this topic focusing on architects. For further information see for example: Moravánszky, Ákos. *Architekturtheorie im 20. Jahrhundert. Eine kritische Anthologie herausgegeben von Ákos Moravánszky.* Vienna: Springer Verlag, 2003.

of pure intuition, which eludes description.[22] The best illustration for this overlapping of interests and theories is provided by a famous, older image from Robert Fludd's (1574–1637) *Utriusque cosmi maioris scilicet et minoris (...) historia* (1619), in which the overlapping of the sensual and the intellectual world, located outside the head and the body, corresponds with the sense and the intellect of the human being in his brain through the five senses. The soul, then, is located where the senses and intellect overlap, along with speculation and thought and memory and motivation. The localization of these functions seems to resonate with the localization of cognitive function in the cerebral cortex, and with the importance of the body in the sense of "embodiment."[23]

All these influences condensed in an intense period of spatial theories. This overview should begin with German doctor and physiologist Johannes Müller (1801–1858), who was one of the first to recognize that perception results from the relationship between nerves and exterior stimuli. Furthermore, he recognized that every sense has a different way of reacting to these stimuli. The consequence he drew from this was far-reaching: the world surrounding us cannot be grasped by our senses objectively. His book, *Handbuch der Physiologie des Menschen* (1838), became a very important reference for proceeding generations of scientists. Among these, the most prominent was German physiologist and physicist Hermann von Helmholtz (1821–1894), a true polymath, whose investigations of optics were groundbreaking and led to a complete understanding of vision. Another physiologist who had great influence in establishing the fundamentals for the discussion of perception was Gustav Theodor Fechner (1801–1887), the founder of *Psychophysik*, a discipline that connects psychology and physics through the possibility of measuring stimuli. In his two primary works, *Elemente der Psychophysik* from 1860 and *Vorschule der Ästhetik* from 1876, he established a series of principles on how the perception of stimuli is structured. He differentiated between intensive and extensive perception—space being an example of the latter—and introduced different types of *Schwellen*: thresholds of perception. The most relevant of these was the "aesthetical threshold," implying the necessity to have both intense and interesting stimuli.[24] Based on the work of Ernst Heinrich Weber (1795–1878) and "Weber's Law" (1834), Fechner established the

so-called "Weber-Fechner Law," which describes how the change of intensity of a stimulus is perceived differently. For example, if one candle is placed next to another one, the change of intensity will be much stronger than if one candle is added to ten others. This law was later extended by Stanley Smith Stevens (1906–1973) into "Steven's Power Law." Fechner also introduced the *Aesthetisches Assoziationsprinzip* (principle of aesthetic association), which implies that our reaction to a stimulus is also dependent on our experience and memory about the object of stimulus. The work of these scientists was paralleled by new insights from psychology, mainly by Wilhelm Wundt (1832–1920)—a student of Helmholz's—and Carl Stumpf (1848–1936). Wundt investigated the relationship between psychology and physiology, and the measurement of stimuli differentiation between qualitative and quantitative dimensions.[25] Among many other things, he researched the relationship of the body to the perception of space, mediated through energy consumption and muscle movement. Stumpf analyzed the perception of space on a more qualitative basis, looking for the mental processes in action there: starting from a whole, space is mentally dissected into its parts. What cannot be differentiated cannot be perceived.[26] Interestingly, Stumpf emphasizes that this act of perception can only take place when standing still, and not when moving. Around this question of how to best perceive space—standing or moving—extreme differences arose.

Building on the vast amount of research into perception, art historians entered the scene, and started applying these principles to the perception of works of art. Friedrich Theodor Vischer (1807–1887) and his son Robert Vischer (1847–1933) were among the first to conduct this transfer, the latter by introducing the notion of *Einfühlung*—literally, empathy: one's own body becomes a datum of the perception of space, which is literally projected onto the space/objects perceived.[27] Their effect will depend on the congruence with the structure of the body and the eye.[28] Interestingly, the elder Vischer represented a nativist, and the younger a cultural explanation of the development of these processes, another topic which is still hotly debated today. This obviously resonates with the recent discovery of "mirror neurons" by a group of Italian scientists.[29]

22 "Space is not a discursive, or as is said, general concept of relations of things in general, but a pure intuition." Kant, Immanuel. *Critique of Pure Reason*, trans. and edited Paul Guyer and Allen W. Wood, Cambridge: Cambridge University Press, 1998, p. 175.
23 "To say that cognition is embodied means that is arises from bodily interactions with the world and is continually meshed with them. From this point of view, therefore, cognition depends on the kinds of experiences that come from having a body with particular perceptual and motor capabilities that are inseparably linked and that together form the matrix within which reasoning, memory, emotion, language and all other aspects of mental life are embedded." Esther Thelen, "Grounded in the World: Developmental Origins of the Embodied Mind." In *Infancy* I (2000), pp. 3–28.
24 Fechner, Gustav Theodor. *Elemente der Psychophysik*. Leipzig 1860.

25 Wundt, Wilhelm. *Grundzüge der Physiologischen Psychologie*. Leipzig: Engelmann, 1874.
26 Stumpf, Carl. *Über den Psychologischen Ursprung der Raumvorstellung*. Leipzig: Verlag von S. Hirzel, 1873.
27 Vischer, Friedrich Theodor. *Ästhetik oder Wissenschaft des Schönen*. Stuttgart: Cotta, 1839.
28 Vischer, Robert. *Über das optische Formgefühl*. Leipzig: Credner, 1873.
29 di Pellegrino G., L. Fadiga, L. Fogassi, V. Galles, and G. Rizzolatti. "Understanding motor events: a neurophhysiological study." In *Experimental Brain Research* 91, Nr. 1, 176–180, 1992.

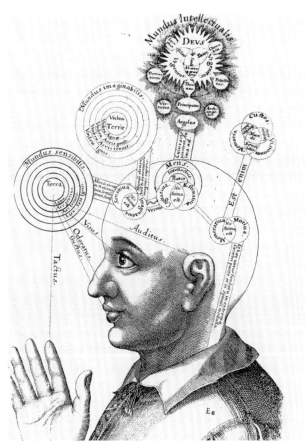

3 Robert Fludd, *Utriusque cosmi maioris scilicet et minoris (...) historia*, 1619

In the wake of the Vischer theories, art historians such as Adolf Hildebrand (1847–1921), Heinrich Wölfflin (864–1945), and August Schmarsow (1853–1936) managed to create a veritable theory of space and perception—although not without major differences in their positions—arriving at Schmarsow's famous definition of architecture as *Raumgestaltung* (the art of shaping space). Schmarsow was among the first to relate spatial perception to the movement of a body inside space. This group extended matters of perception to questions of production, based on the common assumption that only through *making* can one really understand something; that perception is thus part of a process that will result in a work of art. This theory became the most important reference for a generation of architects interested in spatial matters. Nevertheless, this background remained rather speculative, and required another step into the application of the process to design. In this sense, the notion of spatial ability was introduced by architects to describe a specific quality architects possess.[30]

In relation to this, two architects are of particular note:

Theodor Fischer (1862–1938) and Fritz Schumacher, mentioned above. Aside from having been friends, these two architects had a great deal in common: both were important forerunners of modernism and, despite being superseded by modernist heroes, they publicly stood for modernism against Nazism—and not least because of that, they were shunned and pushed into oblivion. Both worked for city administrations and, because of their roles there, they were able to profoundly change the shape of Munich and Hamburg. Both were in direct contact with some of the aforementioned theoreticians of space, primarily Adolf Hildebrand, with whom both were personally acquainted. Both Fischer and Schumacher developed a theory of space based on the perception and transformation of space, and were strongly influenced by their work on the urban scale. This led them to reflect on the differences between form, space, and landscape—also from a historical point of view, as a sequence of convex and concave types of spaces—and to isolate the specificity of architectural and urban space. Yet one important difference remains between the two: while Fischer was a very reserved person—nicknamed "der grosse Schweiger" (the big, silent one)—and wrote very little, Schumacher enjoyed public life and published extensively. For this reason I will discuss Schumacher further, yet one cannot ignore the fact that Fischer was just as relevant for spatial theory.

What thus makes both men so appealing to us—and so different from many other theorists of the time—is that they were not only interested in the point of view of the beholder—"der Betrachtende"—but also the point of view of the designer—"der Schaffende"—as related to the beholder, in the words of Fritz Schumacher. In the former case, one begins by observing a form or space, and tries to delve into the principles that lie behind them; in the second case, one begins in the opposite way: from within, in order to arrive without. As a designer, in the eyes of Schumacher, one must master both.[31]

In his book *Grundlagen der Baukunst. Studien zum Beruf des Architekten* (1916) (Basics of Architecture. Studies in the Profession of Architect), Schumacher delves into the necessary skills an architect must possess and develop, in order to become a "good" architect. He differentiates between *Kennen* (knowing) and *Können* (being able to do). As for knowing, he underscores that every architect needs to possess mathematical thinking and a sense of constructive laws; as for doing, he describes artistic ability and a sense of rhythm, which in the specific case of the architect is based on a sense for the rhythm of spaces.[32] He thus clearly differentiates between an artist and an architect:

---

30 Admittedly, art historians also made reference to spatial ability, such as the previously mentioned Albert Erich Brinckmann, who talks about "Raumsinn"—a sense for space—and made the wonderful statement that still holds true today: "It is hard to talk about the importance of space with those who have no sense for it." Brinckmann, Albert Erich. "Erziehung zum Raumsinn." In *Zeitschrift für Deutschkunde*, Heft 1, 51, 1926.

31 Schumacher, Fritz. "Architektonische Komposition." In *Handbuch der Architektur*. 12. Leipzig: J. M. Gebhardt's Verlag, 1926.

32 In the original German, *Kennen* corresponds to "mathematisches Denken"; *Können* to "künstlerische Begabung" and "rhythmische Gefühlswert." Schumacher, Fritz. *Grundlagen der Baukunst. Studien zum Beruf des Architekten*. Munich: Verlag von Georg D. W. Callwey, 1916, p. 9.

their specific artistic ability is different, based on form and mass for the former and on the relationship of negative and positive space for the latter. The mind of the architect undergoes a specific mental process and is based on a three-dimensional form of imagination: "The capacity to imagine something, at the same time negative and positive, as space and as mass and to transform this conception at will; the capacity to fantasize mass as an organism, quasi-transparent, such that inside and outside are simultaneously present in the imagination; and at the same time movable, such that any thought about a transformation of the interior will immediately affect the exterior: this is what architectonic ability is."[33] The building process, then, is nothing more than the translation of this imagination into the built space of reality. It is clear that Schumacher's preoccupations are less with the process of space perception than with the creation and transformation of space, which makes his theory so valuable for us.

In his most famous essay, published in 1926 as a contribution to *Handbuch der Architektur (Manual of Architecture)*, Schumacher extends and refines his thoughts from 1916. Here, architecture is defined as "the art of a double design, of space and bodies."[34] Architecture is thus neither a question of form nor of space *per se*, but always the result of a combination of the two. At the beginning, there is an architectonic idea, which condenses into a mental image.[35] This is based on the combination of perception and intellect—which cannot be separated—and Schumacher underscores that the perception of space is not only a matter of vision, but of the movement of our bodies.[36] This idea—Schumacher interestingly speaks about an atmosphere, in which the artist resides—then becomes realized through the spaces and bodies of architecture.[37]

These are the references with which students of architecture should be confronted! But over the decades that followed, this knowledge was lost; modernism stigmatized the notion of space in favor of a mechanized, abstract beholder[38]—only to create true masterpieces of a bodily and spatial architecture, such as the Villa Savoye (1931). This is one of the many discrepancies of modernism. Le Corbusier deserves a special mention in this context. Being the shining light of this movement, he radicalized abstraction, in particular by introducing the perspective of the airplane. Yet even in the first issue of the *Esprit Nouveau* from 1920, edited with Amedeé Ozenfant, there is an article by French philosopher Victor Basch on "*L'Esthétique Nouvelle et la Science de l'Art*," (New Aesthetics and the Art of Science) in which some of

the protagonists of the space theories mentioned above are discussed. Thus, Le Corbusier was well aware of this tradition! Later, "space" would resurface in his vocabulary and was accorded an eminent position—without a doubt also influenced by Sigfried Giedion's (1888–1968) book *Space, Time and Architecture: The Growth of a New Tradition* (1941). He even wrote an article for *l'Architecture d'aujourd'hui* with the title "L'espace indicible," or the unspeakable space. This would then be extended in his book, *New World of Space*, published in 1948, which is nothing more than another recollection of his many works, this time under the label of space. Here, Le Corbusier makes statements that would have been unimaginable in previous years: "The essential thing that will be said here is that the release of aesthetic emotion is a special function of space."[39]

Since then, space has resurfaced in many different contexts, in the work of philosophers such as Maurice Merleau-Ponty (1908–1961) and Hermann Schmitz (one should mention also the earlier contribution of Edmund Husserl (1859–1938); architectural historians such as Bruno Zevi (1918–2000); architects such as Geoffrey Scott (1884–1929), Trystan Edwards (1884–1973), Hans van der Laan (1904–1991), Philippe Boudon and Christian de Portzamparc;[40] or media theorists such as Rudolf Arnheim (1904–2007)). This list could obviously be extended at will.

At the beginning of this chapter, we mentioned how a certain degree of irritation was the trigger for our research project and this book. It was an irritation arising from the inability to qualify and quantify "space," as well as the attempts in this direction that were restricted to only architecture or only science.

How often have we come across pseudo-scientific works in architecture that were "neither-nor". Any "incorrect" understanding of references from outside the discipline only make sense when they are integrated into the process of design, rather than remaining mere speculations. Philip Johnson (1906–2005) once made a fantastic comment about the work of Peter Eisenman, regarding his multiple references from philosophy and literary theory: "He's always hiding, hiding behind this web—web is a good word, isn't it? Marvelous word, web. He doesn't really understand Nietzsche. He doesn't understand most of the stuff he spouts. He really is the most tremendous bullshitter. But, and here's the point, he's better than a theorist. He's an artist. But he requires theory to make his art, just like Mies required technology and Hannes Meyer required the proletariat. It's terribly hard to do design. We all need our crutches. And Peter's is his mind."[41]

33 Ibid., p. 25.
34 "Architektur ist die Kunst doppelter Raumgestaltung durch Körpergestaltung." Schumacher, Fritz. "Architektonische Komposition." In *Handbuch der Architektur,* 12. Leipzig: J. M. Gebhardt's Verlag, 1926.
35 Schumacher 1916, p. 44.
36 Schumacher 1926, p. 30.
37 Ibid., p. 45.
38 Taut, Bruno. "Nieder der Seriosismus!" In *Stadtbaukunst alter und neuer Zeit,* 13, Heft 1, 1920.

39 Le Corbusier. *New World of Space.* New York: Reynal & Hitccock, 1948, p. 8.
40 de Portzamparc, Christian, and Philippe Sollers. *Writing and Seeing Architecture.* Minneapolis: University of Minnesota Press, 2002.
41 Philip Johnson, as quoted in: Seabrook, John. "The David Lynch of Architecture." In *Vanity Fair,* 127, January 1991.

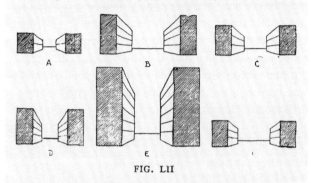

ARCHITECTURAL STYLE

monotony would result if the relation of width of street to height of buildings were to be made constant.

LII E and F represent alternative types of street, each of which is agreeable to the eye. D, however, of square section suffers from the great defect that the parts have not been inflected to take account of their different functions. There is an obvious lack of sensibility if the height of the building has an identical dimension as the width of the street.

The question of the proper framing of by-laws for

FIG. LII

the regulation of street architecture is too large a one to be discussed at length here, but sufficient has perhaps been said to indicate the danger of applying too simple 'rules' to such a subject. A very elaborate code would be necessary if the requirements of hygiene and traffic are to be satisfied without depriving civic architecture of its artistic qualities.

Figs. LIII all have a bearing upon the subject of proportion in architecture. A, a square room, obviously lacks the necessary inflection, because, although its sides are equal and similarly disposed to the cubical content of the room, two sides have windows

118

4 Trystan Edwards, *Diagram*, 1926

So, our irritation is not about the Eisenman-like introduction of references, which are somehow digested and transformed into his projects—nevertheless, the question remains as to whether such references are supposed to influence the spatial effect of a project, as Eisenman sometimes claimed[42]—but about the happy-go-lucky and self-reified flirt of architecture *per se* engaging with something it doesn't truly understand.

42 Gerber, Andri. *Theorie der Städtebaumetaphern. Peter Eisenman und die Utopie der erzählenden Stadt.* Zurich: Chronos, 2012.

THE POTENTIAL OF COGNITIVE SCIENCE FOR ARCHITECTURE

Beatrix Emo and Christoph Hölscher

Introduction

Evaluating what constitutes a good building is a complicated affair. Given that buildings are (often) designed objects, it is important to consider the architect's intentions. Indeed, architects and architectural critics are adept at discussing the various dimensions of what makes good architecture, covering topics such as at what point a building becomes architecture, the aesthetics of buildings, and so forth. However, the architect's intentions are not the only voice to consider when judging what makes a good building. Another useful viewpoint—and one that often remains neglected—is the perspective of the people who use the building. In an ideal scenario, the architect designs a building that fully matches how people eventually use that building once constructed. There are countless examples—even of prize-winning buildings—where this is not the case. It seems that there is a mismatch between the designers' intentions and the end users' experience of the building. One of the aims of the Chair of Cognitive Science at ETH Zurich, a collaborator on the project "How Do Architects 'Think' and Design Space," is to address this mismatch. This chapter aims to elucidate ways in which this mismatch might be tackled, and more generally, to explicate the potential of cognitive science for architectural design.

Spatial Cognition and Architectural Design

Cognitive science is "the study of intelligence and intelligent systems, with particular reference to intelligent behavior as computation."[1] The establishment of the field is often tied to the creation of the journal *Cognitive Science* in 1970, and is comprised of six core disciplines: psychology, computer science, neuroscience, anthropology, linguistics, and philosophy.[2] While architecture is not considered a core contributor to the cognitive science discipline, there is a branch of cognitive science known as "spatial cognition" that is relevant to architecture. Spatial cognition "seeks to understand how humans and other animals perceive, interpret, mentally represent and interact with the spatial

characteristics of their environment."[3] Spatial cognition is a diverse and multidisciplinary field, and is much less well-established than cognitive science; the first handbook to try and document the extent of the field of spatial cognition was published in 2013.[4] The necessity of exploring the intersection between architecture and spatial cognition was born of a desire to examine the human element in architectural design.[5]

The Importance of the User in Architectural Design

Architecture is both an art and a science, not one or the other. As such, it is open to consideration from many different perspectives. Yet cognitive science is not usually one of these. The desire to explore the potential of cognitive science for architecture arose in response to what seemed to be a fundamental lack of consideration for the people who actually use the spaces when they are complete. Although such a lack of consideration is not ubiquitous, as the rise of phenomenology[6] in architecture and architectural sociology[7] demonstrates, work at the intersection of architecture and cognitive science places the end user on an equal footing to architects and buildings, as shown in Figure 1.

---

1   Simon, Herbert Alexander, and Craig A. Kaplan. "Foundations of Cognitive Science." In *Foundations of Cognitive Science*, edited by M.I. Posner. 1–47. Cambridge, MA: MIT Press, 1993.
2   Nunez, Rafael, Michael Allen, Richaed Gao, Carson Miller Rigoli, Josephine Relatord-Doyle, and Arturs Semenuks. "What happened to cognitive science?" In *Nature Human Behavior* 3, 782–719, 2019.

3   Waller, David, and Lynn Nadel. "Introduction: Frameworks for understanding spatial thought (or wrapping our heads around space)." In *Handbook of Spatial Cognition*, edited by D. Waller and L. Nadel, 3–12. Washington, D.C.: American Psychological Association, 2013.
4   Waller, David, and Lynn Nadel. *Handbook of Spatial Cognition*. Washington, D.C.: American Psychological Association, 2013.
5   For a review of current work at the intersection of architecture and spatial cognition see: Mavros, Panagiotis, Rohit K. Dubey, Kristina Jazuk, Hengshan Li, and Christoph Hölscher. "Architectural Psychology for Mixed-Use Cities." In *Future Cities Lab: Indicia 02,* edited by S. Cairns and D. Tunas. Zurich: Lars Müller Publishers, 2019. Emo, Beatrix, Kinda Al-Sayed, and Tasos Varoudis. "Design, cognition and behaviour: Usability in the built environment." In *International Journal of Design, Creativity & Innovation*, 4, No. 2, 63–66, 2016. Conroy Dalton, Ruth, Christoph Hölscher, and Alasdair Turner. "Understanding Space: The Nascent Synthesis of Cognition and the Syntax of Spatial Morphologies:" In *Environment and Planning B: Planning and Design* 39, No. 1, 7–11, 2012.
6   See key texts such as Rasmussen, Steen Eiler. *Experiencing Architecture.* Cambridge, Massachusetts: MIT Press, 195. Norberg-Schulz, Christian. *Genius Loci: Towards a Phenomenology of Architecture.* New York: Rizzoli, 1980. Pallasmaa, Juhani. *The Eyes of the Skin: Architecture and the Senses.* New York: Wiley, 1996/2005. For a review on phenomenology in architecture see Seamon, David. "Phenomenology, place, environment, and architecture: A review of the literature." In *Phenomenology Online*, 36, 1–29, 2000.
7   Several authors have brought together architecture and sociology in their writing. For a review of Lucius Burchkardt's work see: Fezer, Jesko, and Martin Schmitz, eds. *Lucius Burckhardt writings. Rethinking man-made environments: politics, landscape & design.* Basel: Birkhäuser Verlag, 2016. For a different approach bringing together the two fields see Löw, Martina. *The Sociology of Space—Materiality, Social Structures, and Action.* New York, Cultural Sociology: Palgrave Macmillan, 2016.

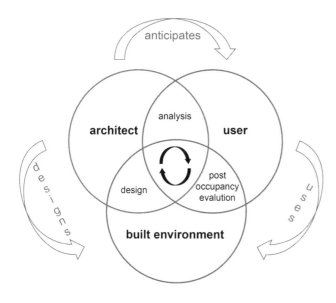

1 Ruth Dalton and Christoph Hölscher, *The Importance of the User in Architectural Design*, 2017

Traditionally, there has been very little place in architecture schools for a discussion of how an eventual end user might experience a proposed design project. Even the term "end user" is entirely external to the language that architects use to discuss their work. Indeed, the term is more common in the commercial world, where meeting the needs of the end user has a monetary value. The term end user also features in some design disciplines, such as product design, and in the broad domain of Human Computer Interaction (HCI). We find the term helpful for several reasons:

1. It refers to the action of being on site.
2. It suggests a relationship between built form and people.
3. It does not exclude the possibility that a building might need to address different types of behavior, which may be born either out of necessity or preference.

By using the term, we affirm that it is paramount to discuss how people behave in buildings, and that such behavior should be intrinsic to the architectural discourse.

Evidence-Based Design Methods

Over the last two decades, there has been a concerted effort to explore the different facets of user-oriented architecture. Such efforts have been led by interdisciplinary academic centers worldwide, such as the Transregional Collaborative Research Center SFB/TR 8 Spatial Cognition in Germany—which was superseded by the Bremen Spatial Cognition Center (BSCC)—or the Spatial Intelligence and Learning Center (SILC) in the USA, along with individual research groups (of which the Chair of Cognitive Science at ETH Zurich is but one) and several architectural consultancies (such as Space Syntax Ltd., Spacelab, Spacescape, etc.). Many architectural studios, such as KCAP and UN Studio, have also adopted methods that unpack how people behave in space, although access to any such approaches is often confidential.[8]

A keystone to the success of user-centric approaches has been the integration of methods from different fields, such as cognitive science. Such mixed-method approaches fall under the term "evidence-based" design methods.[9] Examples of the types of methods that can be used to inform evidence-based design are behavioral observations, questionnaire and interview data, visibility analysis and space syntax, or simulation and agent-based modeling, as well as behavioral experiments more generally. The methods can then be used to elucidate the human element in architectural and urban design.[10]

While there is a substantial critical mass of researchers and practitioners adopting such methods, they are not yet mainstream. This is because there are several limiting factors preventing the widespread adoption of evidence-based design methods in architectural design.[11] Two of the major challenges are that the correct implementation of such methods takes time and requires specific knowledge. For example, practices may wish to collect behavioral data about how people use an existing space, but to collect enough data, systematically, takes time. Another option may be to use simulation tools to predict how people might behave in a space, but these simulation tools tend to use different software from the typical CAD programs used by designers, which poses several challenges: lengthy import/export pipelines, for example, make it cumbersome to test sequential design iterations; or running simulations and evaluating results requires the kind of specific knowledge often gained through training (e.g. master's level courses for architects). Despite these limitations, evidence-based design methods have been useful in illuminating the human element in real case studies, as discussed below in reference to the Seattle Central Library.

8   See the following presentations, given as part of the "Evidence-Based Design: Methods and Tools For Evaluating Architectural Design" course module at the Chair of Cognitive Science, ETH Zurich: Ute Schneider, "Humanscale, Urbanscale. Flows: mobility and accessibility as driver for density, intensity and urbanity", presentation (28 November 2017), ETH Zurich, Switzerland; Veddeler, Christian. "Motion Matters: Systems Thinking in Architecture," presentation (3 December 2019) at ETH Zurich, Switzerland.

9   For a discussion of the use of the term "evidence-based methods" in architecture, see Emo, Beatrix. "Why evidence-based design methods are useful for architectural design." In *Research Culture in Architecture: Cross-disciplinary collaboration*, edited by Christopher Robelle, Cornelie Leopold, and Ulrike Weber, 173–182. Basel: Birkhäuser Verlag, 2019.

10 For a recent discussion of how such methods are being applied in research on mixed-use cities see Panagiotis Mavros et al., 2019 (see note 5).

11 For a discussion see Emo, Beatrix. "Why evidence-based design methods are useful for architectural design." In *Research Culture in Architecture: Cross-disciplinary collaboration*, edited by Christopher Robelle, Cornelie Leopold, and Ulrike Weber, 173–182. Basel: Birkhäuser Verlag, 2019.

Case Study: Seattle Central Library

The renowned Seattle Central Library building was designed by the Office of Metropolitan Architects (OMA) and Loschky, Marquardt, and Nesholm Architects (LMN), and opened in 2004. The building has won several accolades (e.g. American Library Association's best reviewed building in 2005).[12] It is also a building that is difficult to navigate.[13] The alignment between these two elements—a prize-winning design on the one hand, and a building that is difficult to navigate on the other hand—poses a challenge. This is because of the underlying assumption, shared by many, that a public library should be easy to navigate. An interdisciplinary research team used a wealth of different methods to uncover the complexity of the building and to see how that complexity matches—or fails to match—how users experience the building.[14] This research shows that users' needs are not met in regard to navigability, because they report frustration when walking through the building and way-finding performance to key destinations is low. The work on the Seattle Central Library has done much to uncover how a prize-winning, complex building is perceived by its users. What remains missing is a debate on whether that specific building—public libraries, or public buildings more generally—*should* be navigable. Cognitive scientists, architectural researchers, and designers may have differing opinions on this matter. As more work is done at the intersection of architecture and psychology, a critical discourse should be developed as to whether (public) buildings should be navigable.

Looking Ahead: the Potential of Cognitive Science for Architecture

The cognitive revolution of the 1950s and 1960s impacted many fields, including architecture. Over the past twenty years or more, research at the intersection of cognitive science and architecture has sought to better understand how users experience the built environment. This has been done for both architectural and urban-scale case studies. Such research has identified potential synergies at the intersection between these two fields, but much more work must be done. Despite the development of an evidence-based design toolkit, these methods are rarely implemented during the design process. One way of tackling this is to embed such methods into the architectural curriculum.[15] Another challenge is to develop tools that can be used seamlessly by the designer during the design process, without the need for lengthy import/export procedures; this would allow such methods to be implemented iteratively. Findings from the courses taught at the Chair of Cognitive Science over the last five years suggest that evidence-based design methods work well when used iteratively, and is most effective as a design-analysis feedback loop—meaning that each step in the design process is informed by the findings from previously undertaken analyses (as shown by the arrows in the central part of Figure 1). Finally, more work needs to be done exploring how the knowledge developed by interdisciplinary research teams can be best distilled for practitioners, so that the next generation of architects can profit from the advances of cognitive science for architecture.

12 American Library Association, AIA/ALA Library Buildings Award 2005 and 2007, http://www.ala.org/llama/awards/aiaalalibrarybuildings (accessed November 11, 2019).

13 Robin Pogrebin, Inside the year's best reviewed buildings, *The New York Times* (26 December 2004), https://www.nytimes.com/2004/12/26/arts/design/inside-the-years-bestreviewed-buildings.html (accessed 11 November 2019).

14 Conroy Dalton, Ruth, and Christoph Hölscher. *Take One Building. Interdisciplinary Research Perspectives of the Seattle Central Library*. Abingdon, Oxon: Routledge, 2017. Kuliga, Saskia F., Benjamin Nelligan, Ruth Conroy Dalton, Steven Marchette, Amy L. Shelton, Laura Carlson, and Christoph Hölscher. "Exploring Individual Differences and Building Complexity in Wayfinding: The Case of the Seattle Central Library." In *Environment and Behavior* 51, No. 5, 622–665, 2019.

15 Emo, Beatrix, and Christoph Hölscher. "Evidence-Based Design Thinking:" *ETH Zurich Innoview*, https://staging.innoview.pbdev.ch/project/evidence-based-design-thinking/ (accessed 11 November 2019).

GENDER DIFFERENCES IN SPATIAL ABILITIES AND STEM PARTICIPATION

Michal Berkowitz and Elsbeth Stern

An underrepresentation of women in the fields of science, technology, engineering, and mathematics (STEM) has been known to researchers and educators for many decades. Although there has been an overall increase in the share of women entering STEM fields since the 1970s, it has been relatively slow. In some fields, for example in engineering and computer science, it remains low and has hardly changed since the 1990s.[1] This situation has raised substantial social and economic concern regarding the conditions that bring about uneven gender-by-field distributions, especially considering that women are no less intellectually capable than men of learning and achieving in these fields.[2] Consequently, extensive research is being done on gender issues in educational and vocational contexts in the sub-domains of psychology as well as in educational science and sociology.

One area of gender differences that has received much empirical attention in the context of STEM learning is performance on spatial ability tests. Whereas, in most areas of cognitive performance, no substantial gender differences emerge,[3] some types of spatial ability tests consistently yield robust gender differences favoring male participants.[4] The most frequent finding is on tasks involving mental rotation: the ability to mentally visualize rotational movement of objects, for example, in order to judge whether objects are structurally identical or mirror images of one another. This ability is typically assessed by the classical Mental Rotations Test,[5] although variations of this test and other types of stimuli also exist for children. A large body of research has replicated a male advantage on mental rotation tasks both among children and adults, across cultures, as well as across areas of expertise.[6] Why do women perform less well than men on some tests of spatial ability? Answers to this question range from biologically-based reasons, including genetic and hormonal influences, to social-environmental origins, such as gendered play and experiences.[7] For example, some types of child play, such as construction toys or some computer games, have been positively linked with mental rotation ability, and are also stereotyped as masculine activities.[8]

Because the cultural and social environment influences children's preferences, the argument is that boys and girls accumulate different experiences from an early age, which have consequences for the skills they develop. Many researchers acknowledge that multiple factors interact in creating spatial gender gaps, though it is somewhat more difficult to determine the relative contribution of each factor. Nonetheless, evidence from twin studies does suggest that a larger portion of variance in spatial performance is explained by environmental factors than by genetic factors, both among girls and boys.[9] Such findings are interesting not only from a pure cognitive perspective, but also because of their potential implications for academic and vocational achievements, particularly in the STEM fields. Specifically, since spatial thinking is relevant to many STEM subjects, including engineering, chemistry, geoscience, mathematics, medicine, and of course architecture, spatial abilities are regarded as important skills for succeeding in these fields. The role of spatial abilities, as assessed by standard measures, is regarded to be most important at the beginner level, when students still lack domain-specific knowledge and skills.[10]

1   Ceci, Stephen J., Donna K. Ginther, Shulamit Kahn, and Wendy M. Williams. "Women in academic science: A changing landscape." In *Psychological Science in the Public Interest*, 15, No. 3, 75–141, 2014.

2   Lindberg, Sara M., Janet Shibley Hyde, Jennifer Petersen, and Marcia C. Linn. "New trends in gender and mathematics performance: A meta-analysis." In *Psychological Bulletin* 136, No. 6 (2010), pp. 1123–1135. Strand, Steve, Ian J. Deary, and Pauline Smith. "Sex differences in cognitive abilities test scores: A UK national picture." In *British Journal of Educational Psychology* 76, No. 3, 463–480, 2006.

3   Ceci et al. 2014 (see note 1); Shipley Hyde, Janet. "The gender similarities hypothesis." In *American Psychologist*, 60, No. 6, 581, 2005.

4   Levine, Susan Cohen, Alana Dulaney, Stella F. Lourenco, Stacy Ehrlich, and Kristin Ratliff. "Sex differences in spatial cognition: Advancing the conversation." In *Wiley Interdisciplinary Reviews: Cognitive Science* 7, No. 2, 127–155, 2016. Linn, Marcia C., and Anne C. Petersen. "Emergence and characterization of sex differences in spatial ability: A meta-analysis." In *Child Development,* 1479–1498, 1985. Voyer, Daniel, Susan Voyer, and Philip Bryden. "Magnitude of sex differences in spatial abilities: a meta-analysis and consideration of critical variables." In *Psychological Bulletin*, 117, No. 2, 250, 1995.

5   Vandenberg, Steven G., and Allan R. Kuse. "Mental Rotations, a Group Test of Three-Dimensional Spatial Visualization." In *Perceptual and Motor Skills* 47, No. 2, 599–604, 1978.

6   Levine et al., 2016 (see note 4); Peters, Michael, Wolfgang Lehmann, Sayuri Takahira, Yoshiaki Takeuchi, and Kirsten Jordan. "Mental rotation test performance in four cross-cultural samples (n= 3367): overall sex differences and the role of academic program in performance." In *Cortex* 42, No. 7, 1005–1014, 2006.

7   See Levine et al., 2016 for a detailed review (see note 4).

8   Quaiser-Pohl, Claudia M., Christian Geiser, and Wolfgang Lehmann. "The relationship between computer-game preference, gender, and mental-rotation ability." In *Personality and Individual Differences* 40, No. 3, 609–619, 2006. Terlecki, Melissa S., and Nora Newcombe. "How important is the digital divide? The relation of computer and videogame usage to gender differences in mental rotation ability." In *Sex Roles* 53, No. 5–6, 433–441, 2005. Weisgram, Erica S., and Lisa M. Dinella, *Gender typing of children's toys: How Early Play Experiences Impact Development.* Washington, D.C.: American Psychological Association, 2018.

9   Tosto, Maria Grazia, Ken Benjamin Hanscombe, Claire M.A. Haworth, Oliver S.P. Davis, Stephen Petrill, Philip S. Dale, Sergey Malykh, Robert Plomin, and Yulia Kovas. "Why do spatial abilities predict mathematical performance?" In *Developmental Science* 17, No. 3, 462–470, 2014.

10 Uttal, David H., and Cheryl Ann Cohen. "Spatial Thinking and STEM Education." In *Psychology of Learning and Motivation*, Vol. 57, 147–181. Amsterdam: Elsevier, 2012.

Additionally, spatial abilities have been marked as long-term predictors of academic success in STEM subjects, in addition to other predictors such as verbal and mathematical abilities.[11] It is therefore not surprising that gender differences in spatial abilities are considered one of the contributing factors to the underrepresentation of women in STEM fields, but there is controversy over the degree to which spatial gender gaps can explain STEM gender gaps.[12] Nonetheless, comprehensive accounts of the underrepresentation problem usually include gender differences in spatial abilities as one of several factors to be taken into account.[13]

One aspect that is less debatable is that spatial abilities can be improved by training.[14] There have been numerous studies showing that practicing and training spatial ability tasks, particularly over extended time periods, lead to clear gains in spatial performance. Such gains are most evident for tasks similar to those included in the training, although some effects can generalize to different spatial tasks. In one example, undergraduate students either trained mental rotation with a computer game or repeated the same mental rotation test several times over a period of twelve weeks.[15] Both types of training led to long-term improvements in mental rotation performance, and those who trained with a computer game showed transfer effects to other spatial ability tasks. With respect to gender, both men and women showed improved performance, though the rate of change depended on their prior experience with spatial tasks: women with low levels of spatial experience showed slower improvement in the early phase of the intervention, and more pronounced improvement in later phases, compared to men and women with high levels of spatial experience. Another example is the work led by Sheryl Sorby, who developed an extensive spatial training program aimed at first-year engineering students with low levels of spatial skills—a group with proportionally more women than men.[16] This intervention was given as a weekly course, in which students worked through exercises requiring different types of spatial visualization (such as rotations, cross-sections, orthographic projections). The course led to significant improvements on spatial tasks performance and, additionally, students who participated in the course achieved higher grades in engineering graphics courses compared to students who were not exposed to the training. In light of these findings, one potential path to reducing spatial gender differences is through training and practice of spatial skills. In particular, given that men and women accumulate different levels of experience with spatial tasks before they attend higher education, an opportunity for spatial training at the beginning of higher education studies may enable students to advance more rapidly in spatially demanding fields, such as engineering and architecture. However, since spatial training affects both women and men to a similar extent, improving spatial skills through training may not eliminate gender gaps if both genders are given the opportunity to train.[17] Nevertheless, it may be more important to improve initially underdeveloped spatial skills up to a certain level, thus reaching a better starting point, regardless of whether gender gaps remain or not.

This last point leads us to several unanswered questions regarding the link between gender gaps in spatial abilities and STEM gender gaps. First, it is not clear if women's lower performance on some spatial tasks is a reason why they are less well-represented in STEM fields and drop out of STEM at higher rates in advanced stages. A clear and direct link between psychometric spatial abilities showing gender differences and domain-specific achievements—such as success in specific STEM courses or vocational positions—has not been clearly established. In fact, some of the studies that examined spatial abilities of experts found that they develop specialized skills for their fields rather than rely on general spatial abilities, such as those assessed by standardized tests.[18]

Thus, one may wonder whether studying a spatially demanding field such as architecture does not, in and of itself, provide the necessary training for the profession. In order to justify spatial training as a means to reduce STEM gender gaps, one would need to show that initial gender differences in spatial abilities lead to women failing to fulfill their potential in the field. Of course, given the positive effects of spatial training, one could choose to provide such training regardless of gender, as an efficient way to "boost" students' initial spatial skills, assuming these are relevant to the profession.

Additionally, it is not clear which level of spatial abilities would be needed for successful STEM learning, and whether

11 Wai, Jonathan, David Lubinski, and Camilla P. Benbow. "Spatial ability for STEM domains: Aligning over 50 years of cumulative psychological knowledge solidifies its importance." In *Journal of Educational Psychology* 101, No. 4, 817–835, 2009.

12 Ceci et al., 2014 (see note 1).

13 Halpern, Diane, Camilla P. Benbow, David C. Geary, Ruben Gur, Janet Shibley Hyde, and Morton Ann Gernsbacher. "The Science of Sex Differences in Science and Mathematics." In *Psychological Science in the Public Interest* 8, No. 1, 1–51, 2007.

14 Baenninger, Maryann, and Nora Newcombe. "The role of experience in spatial test performance: A meta- analysis." In *Sex Roles* 20, No. 5–6, 327–344, 1989. Uttal, David H., Nathaniel G. Meadow, Elizabeth Tipton, Linda L. Hand, Alison R. Alden, Christopher Warren, and Nora S. Newcombe. "The malleability of spatial skills: A meta-analysis of training studies." In *Psychological Bulletin* 139, 352–402, 2013.

15 Terlecki, Melissa S., Nora S. Newcombe, and Michelle Little. "Durable and generalized effects of spatial experience on mental rotation: Gender differences in growth patterns." In *Applied Cognitive Psychology: The Official Journal of the Society for Applied Research in Memory and Cognition* 22, No. 7, 996–1013, 2008.

16 Sorby, Sheryl. "Developing 3D spatial skills for engineering students." In *Australasian Journal of Engineering Education* 13, No. 1, 1–11, 2007. Sorby, Sheryl, Beth M. Casey, Norma Veurink, and Alana Dulaney. "The role of spatial training in improving spatial and calculus performance in engineering students." In *Learning and Individual Differences* 26, 20–29, 2013. Sorby, Sheryl, and Beverly J. Baartmans. "The Development and Assessment of a Course for Enhancing the 3-D Spatial Visualization Skills of First Year Engineering Students." In *Journal of Engineering Education* 89, No. 3, 301–307, 2000.

17 Baenninger and Newcombe, 1989 (see note 14); Levine et al., 2016 (see note 4).

18 Stieff, Mike, Minjung Ryu, Bonnie Dixon, and Mary Hegarty. "The Role of Spatial Ability and Strategy Preference for Spatial Problem Solving in Organic Chemistry." In *Journal of Chemical Education* 89, No. 7 854–859, 2012.

it has some threshold. Considering that gender differences in spatial abilities remain when both genders are trained, what implication could this have on gender gaps in academic and occupational achievement? One hypothesis could be that—because an advantage for males on spatial tasks is preserved—a male advantage in achievement will also be preserved. However, this is by no means the only hypothesis. The case may be that beyond some level of spatial ability, gender differences in tasks such as mental rotation would no longer matter for performance on field-specific tasks, because with sufficient expertise, both genders develop the necessary skills for such tasks. As previously, mentioned, spatial abilities are not the sole, or even the central, reason for an underrepresentation of women in STEM. Rather, even with a STEM-suitable cognitive profile—which includes both high mathematical and spatial ability—women choose to specialize in STEM subjects less frequently than men with a similar profile.[19] Researchers have pointed to many factors other than abilities or skills that play a role in academic and vocational gender gaps, including self-concept, interests, ability beliefs, and gender stereotypes.[20]

In summary, gender gaps clearly exist in participation rates in some STEM fields. Gender differences also clearly exist in performance on some types of spatial tasks. Research suggests that the latter is one factor out of many that may play a role creating the first. As the focus of this book is on architecture, we conclude with some remarks regarding this particular field. Architecture is occasionally classified as a STEM discipline, but it also belongs to the realm of art. Comparing the gender distribution in male-dominated STEM fields, women participate in architectural studies at higher rates, as much as 40% to 50% of the student body at the undergraduate level, and only slightly less at the graduate level.[21] However, as in other disciplines, the proportion of women in architecture tends to drop as one ascends educational and vocational levels. As with other STEM fields, architecture has traditionally been a male-dominated profession, and still seems to be perceived as such today.[22] Although few would disagree that architects should have good spatial skills, there are surely more characteristics that contribute to making a "good architect." Moreover, as discussed above, gender gaps on spatial ability tests do not necessarily indicate gender gaps in domain-specific perfor-

mance, and thus cannot, in and of themselves, fully explain gender gaps on academic or vocational levels. Women in architecture may face various obstacles unrelated to cognitive ability in this profession.[23] Currently, less research seems to be done in this area compared to other STEM fields. The gender differences in spatial tests performance found in the research described in this book are consistent with findings from research in other populations. We think their implications on the professional development of both women and men in architecture are not yet clear. In order to fully evaluate gender disparities in architecture, future research would need to include measures other than cognitive abilities, as well as to follow students systematically through key milestones in their careers.

19 Dekhtyar, Serhiy, Daniela Weber, Jonas Helgertz, and Agneta Herlitz. "Sex differences in academic strengths contribute to gender segregation in education and occupation: A longitudinal examination of 167,776 individuals." In *Intelligence* 67, 84–92, March 2018.

20 Ceci et al., 2014 (see note 1).

21 ETH Zurich, Gender Monitoring Report 2018/2019, https://ethz.ch/services/en/employment-and-work/working-environment/equal-opportunities/strategie-und-zahlen/gender-monitoring.html (accessed 19 November 2019); Association of Collegiate Schools of Architecture, Where are the Women? Measuring Progress on Gender in Architecture (October 2014), http://www.acsa-arch.org/resources/data-resources/women (accessed 19 November 2019).

22 Kuhlmann, Dörte. *Gender studies in architecture: space, power and difference.* Abingdon: Routledge 2014.

23 Ibid.

MULTIPLE INTELLIGENCES THEORY AND ARCHITECTURAL EDUCATION

Peter Holgate

Art and design subjects, including architecture, have traditionally attracted students with aptitudes and skills that are not necessarily acknowledged or appreciated by the dominant text-based learning and teaching methods employed in the majority of secondary or university-level curricula. An entrenched preference to assess verbal and written skills consequently misses the additional evaluation of attributes and abilities that may contribute to a scholar's academic profile and potential. In response to this hegemonic state, Howard Gardner's theory of "multiple intelligences" seeks to acknowledge and categorize a more comprehensive consideration of functional, affective, creative, and applicative skills.[1] Gardner's original theory separates a normative, singular conceptualization of intelligence into eight discrete "modalities" that may more accurately reflect the range of abilities required for full human functionality:

1) musical-rhythmic, 2) visual-spatial, 3) verbal-linguistic, 4) logical-mathematical, 5) bodily-kinesthetic, 6) interpersonal, 7) intrapersonal, 8) naturalistic.

In terms of educational development, traditional teaching and learning approaches tend to favor teaching and assessment methods that focus on "verbal-linguistic" and "logical-mathematical" modalities. Evaluation of human capacities in the other six fields appears to be relatively under-represented. Therefore, the research project "How do architects think and design space?" conducted at the ZHAW and ETH Zurich, holds the promise of multiple benefits for enhancing educational approaches, particularly in the development of objective methods of evaluating visual-spatial intelligence and abilities. This initiative has particular value for the development and assessment of spatial, perceptual, and problem-solving skills within architectural design. Principally, this research tool can be used to evaluate the existing abilities of participants and students, in order to interpret two-dimensional information as three-dimensional models (and vice versa); to mentally rotate three-dimensional forms and to visualize such volumes from alternative perspectives; and, in architectural terms, to correlate plans, sections, and elevations from singular two-dimensional forms. Identification of such "visual-spatial" intelligence may provide an initial indication of participants' potentials for design thinking, visualization skills, and three-dimensional creativity, with the potential to predict possible success in both current and future professions that demand key skills such as deductive reasoning and complex problem solving.[2] The empirical methodology employed in the online evaluation may also provide an empirical alternative to the subjective "connoisseurship" models of assessment that still prevail in arts and design education,[3] having a potential application to identify untapped spatial intelligence capacities at the outset of a student's education.

Additionally, the longitudinal nature of this inquiry provides an opportunity to test whether such "visual-spatial" intelligence is developed or enhanced through the normative methods of architectural design education. Such a transformative impact would appear to be an intrinsic aim of such pedagogies.[4] The National Architectural Accrediting Board, responsible for validation of courses of architecture in the USA, demands that curricula develop "graduates with an understanding of design as a multidimensional process involving problem resolution and the discovery of new opportunities."[5] Section A of this document, entitled "Critical Thinking and Representation," concerns student performance criteria, and pays particular heed to the student's acuity with two- and three-dimensional design skills.[6] However, in seeking to achieve these learning outcomes, architectural education tends to remain uncritically wedded to many traditions of nineteenth-century Beaux-Arts studio teaching methods.[7] A systematic and objective evaluation of whether these traditional methods actually

2   Bakhshi, Hasan, Jonathan M. Downing, Michael A. Osborne, and Philippe Schneider. *The Future of Skills: Employment in 2030*. London: Pearson and Nesta, 2004, p. 67.
3   Webster, Helena. "The Assessment of Design Project Work (Summative Assessment, Briefing Guide No. 09)." (1 March 2007), https://www.heacademy.ac.uk/knowledge-hub/assessment-design-project-work-summative-assessment-briefing-guide-no-09 (accessed: 30 July 2019).
4   Mezirow, Jack, and Edward W. Taylor. *Transformative Learning in Practice: Insights from Community, Workplace and Higher Education*. San Francisco: Jossey-Bass, 2009.
5   National Architectural Accrediting Board (NAAB) (2014) "2014 Conditions for Accreditation" (18 July 2014) https://www.naab.org/wp-content/uploads/01_Final-Approved-2014-NAAB-Conditions-for-Accreditation-2.pdf (accessed 24 July 2019), p. 11.
6   Ibid., p. 16.
7   Dutton, Thomas A. (ed.). *Voices in Architectural Education: Cultural Politics and Pedagogy*. New York: Bergin & Garvey, 1991. McClean, David. "Embedding Learner Independence in Architecture Education: Reconsidering Design Studio Pedagogy." PhD thesis (Robert Gordon University, 2009). Doidge, Charles, Rosie Parnell, Rachel Sara, and Mark Parsons. *The Crit. An Architecture Student's Handbook: Seriously Useful Guides*. Oxford: Architectural Press, 2006. Stevens, Garry. *The Favored Circle: The Social Foundations of Architectural Distinction*. Cambridge, MA: MIT Press, 1998.

1   Gardner, Howard. *Frames of Mind: The Theory of Multiple Intelligences*. New York: Basic Books, 2004.

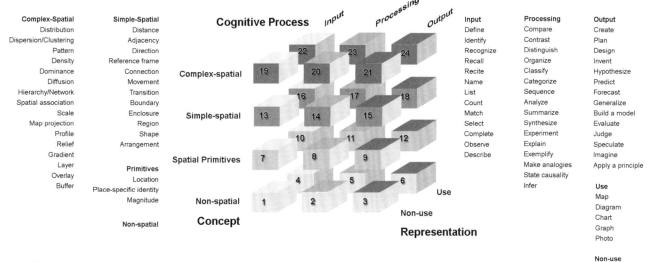

1 Taxonomy of Spatial Thinking by Jo and Bednarz, 2009

improve the spatial intelligence of students over the course of their studies is long overdue; utilizing this tool could complement the few comparable inquiries that foray into this territory.[8]

As an overarching theme, the development of this tool provides a wide-ranging assessment strategy that directly evaluates spatial intelligence through disciplinary-appropriate visual methodologies,[9] thereby acknowledging the authentic application of multiple intelligences within architectural design.[10] This visual focus has particular value with respect to students with dyslexia and other similar neurological conditions, who may not excel in the evaluation of "verbal-linguistic" skills, but who may well be capable of excellence in art, architectural design, and visual communication.[11] Fitzwater illuminates the "emancipatory" possibilities inherent in unlocking the untapped potential of students who are deemed to "fail" by normative and narrow educational approaches. Imaginative, student-centered methods of teaching, learning, and assessment serve to democratize opportunities for learning and development through a sophisticated appreciation of the diversity of academic literacies and individuated talents.[12]

Discussion

The ZHAW and ETH Zurich inquiry, assessment, and training tool provides a valuable addition to ongoing discussions of spatial cognition and spatial intelligence. Participant engagement is enhanced by the problem-based "gamification" of the evaluation, and the range of assessment tasks within the test span a variety of abilities and academic challenges. In future iterations, this methodology could seek to discern increasingly sophisticated academic levels of spatial intelligence, as categorized in Jo and Bednarz's conceptualization of a taxonomy of spatial thinking.[13] An ethical issue arises with the potential to use this tool to evaluate the potential of prospective and new students of architecture, regarding whether or not they have the spatial intelligence and abilities to succeed in architectural education (and therefore whether they are admitted into such courses of study). However, the longitudinal nature of the study also seeks to uncover whether spatial intelligence can successfully be developed over several years of study, possibly balancing out this potentially negative consequence.

In contrast, this paper argues that the inquiry's visual methodologies to evaluate spatial cognizance provides a model of emancipatory assessment, in that it aligns with a "multiple intelligences" approach that could benefit non-traditional students, particularly those with neurodiverse profiles that are hindered by normative educational models. In similar fashion, it could be argued that a multiple-intelligences approach to architectural and arts education could well encompass many more of Garner's "modalities" to successfully reflect the complexity of the discipline and the diversity of its practices.[14]

8   Mostafa, Magda, and Hoda Mostafa. "How do Architects Think? Learning Styles and Architectural Education." In *International Journal of Architectural Research* 4, No. 2, 310–317, July 2010.

9   Rose, Gillian. *Visual Methodologies: An Introduction to Researching with Visual Materials.* London: SAGE, 2016.

10 D'Souza, Newton. "Design Intelligences: a Case for Multiple Intelligences in Architectural Design." In *ArchNet-IJAR: International Journal of Architectural Research* 1, No. 2, 15–34, July 2007.

11 Fitzwater, Lynda. "Theory and Practice in Art & Design education and Dyslexia: The emancipatory potentials of a neurodiversity framework." In *Humana.Mente Journal of Philosophical Studies* 11, No. 33, 121–143, 2018. Holgate, Peter. "Developing an inclusive curriculum of architecture for students with dyslexia." In *Art, Design & Communication in Higher Education* 14, No.1, 87–99, July 2015.

12 Dewey, John. *Democracy and Education: An Introduction to the Philosophy of Education.* London: Simon & Brown, 2011. Freire, Paulo. *Pedagogy of the Oppressed.* New York: Continuum, 2000.

13 Jo, Injeong, and Sarah Witham Bednarz. "Evaluating Geography Textbook Questions from a Spatial Perspective: Using Concepts of Space, Tools of Representation, and Cognitive Processes to Evaluate Spatiality." In *Journal of Geography* 108, No. 1, 4–13, 2009.

14 Clarke, Angela, and Peter Cripps. "Fostering Creativity: A Multiple Intelligences Approach to Designing Learning in Undergraduate Fine Art." In *International Journal of Art & Design Education* 31, No. 2, 113–126, June 2012.

TRAINING SPATIAL ABILITIES?

Detlef Schulz

1 Representation of Euclid

Space in the Euclidean sense[1] is fascinating—it is simultaneously immaterial while also being an essential part of our material world. Space wants to be conceived and planned, just as it wants to be experienced and used. As an architectural space—a space of utility—it fulfills more primary human needs than simply eating, drinking, and breathing. Without the natural spaces created by humans—and/or those which they appropriate and shape—significant portions of the earth would simply be uninhabitable. Buildings provide protection and security from the brute forces of a hostile environment. Despite their immateriality, spaces can be entered, walked through, and measured in their length, width, and height. Like modeling clay, they can be pressed, stretched, bent, separated, lined up, or stacked on top of one another. However, in contrast to clay, their immateriality also allows them to be superimposed—a spatial phenomenon that Robert Slutzky (1929-2005) and Colin Rowe (1920-1999) described in their essay "Transparency."[2] Although, in fact, it is not visible at all, space is both quantitatively as well as qualitatively measurable, an object of desire, and it can be sold. As a product, space is not a quantitatively and qualitatively describable "thing" that is tangible in the physical sense; rather, it can be grasped intellectually, through spatial imagination.

It is therefore difficult to understand how space is conceived and perceived, because strictly speaking, one can only recognize the boundaries of space—its material trappings—rather than the thing itself. The material limitations of observable, walkable, and usable space are the primary elements separating it from its immediate surroundings. Along with the distinctive qualities of size and design, these elements generate an atmosphere, in which a space's *appearance* is actually projected onto the (transparent) space, resulting in its specific DNA. Because space does not appear as an object, but must be derived from the object (the spatial boundary), the observation of space is neither banal nor self-evident. It is not imperative that a perceived space must be enclosed on all sides: consider, for example, the *courtyard of honor* bordered on three sides, or the type of loggia spanned between floor and ceiling. In his scientific-physiological studies on the observation of art, Adolf

Hildebrand (1847-1921)[3] goes even further, asserting that even a central object such as a rock, tree, or building can "gather around itself" a space, generating its surroundings. Even though an architect is typically considered to be a specialist in space, it is important to remember that architecture is by no means the only discipline that grapples with spatial phenomena. Art, photography, film, as well as music, dance, theater, literature, and philosophy—and even mathematics, physics, and other natural sciences—deal with abstract concepts of space in the broadest sense. Architectural spaces primarily differ from those of the other disciplines in regard to their utility, which constitutes the specific architectural aspect of a space, regardless of whether it is an exterior or an interior space. They also differ from the exterior and interior spaces existing in nature, because they are deliberately and artificially produced. Therefore, it is first the idea of creation and second the idea of utility that differentiates architectural space—whether built or not—from both nature and the other disciplines that deal with space in the broadest sense. Neither the idea of *venustas* (design) nor the idea of *firmitas* (construction) in the Vitruvian Triangle[4] distinguish architectural creations from those of the other space-defining disciplines. These, too, engage with dimensions, structures, constructions, proportions, rhythms—the essential tools of design—but it is the idea of *utilitas* (utility),

---

1 See the concept of Euclidian space in Book 11 of Euclid's *Elements*, translated by Thomas L. Heath (Santa Fe, NM: Green Lion Press, 2017).

2 Rowe, Colin, and Robert Slutzky. *Transparency. With a commentary by Bernard Hoesli and an introduction by Werner Oechslin.* Basel/Boston/Berlin: Birkhäuser Verlag, 1997.

3 von Hildebrand, Adolf. *The Problem of Form in Painting and Sculpture.* New York, NY: G. E. Stechert & Company, 1907.

4 Vitruvius. *Ten Books on Architecture.* translated by Morris Hickey Morgan, Cambridge, MA: Harvard University Press, 1914.

or ultimately, the human requirements of comfort, that makes architecture unique within the space-defining realms of art, the humanities, and the natural sciences.

All of the aforementioned disciplines have developed their own specific tools with which to measure and reproduce space, such that they can capture the specific attributes of the general concept of space necessary to exercise their profession. In our discipline, these tools are sketches, drawings, images, and volumetric or spatial models. In the future, through the use of new computer-aided representational possibilities, film could also become a media with which to better understand perception in motion. These instruments can be divided into two categories: the *planimetric* and the *spatial*. Above all, planimetric images—projections of space-defining elements onto horizontal and vertical planes (sections and elevations)—serve to provide objectivity and comparability for scalar objects. But they also act as a means of representation with which to produce the parts necessary to construct a building. Three-dimensional images of space (images or models, real or virtual) serve to represent a spatial effect, and are therefore anything but objective. This is because the choice of the focal point alone—or choice of location in an image or model view—allows for an infinite number of manipulations, aside from the further creative possibilities generated by determining the direction of the perspective view (horizontal, worm's eye, and bird's eye), angle (from wide-angle to telephoto lens), and illumination (diffuse to directional light, bright to dark, from ambient lighting to sidelighting and backlighting).

Regardless of which means of representation we utilize to present architectural space, the fact remains that spatial imagination must precede technical implementation or production—and every representational possibility has this in common. If the space to be represented is an existing (real) space, the "observation-imagination" is at work; however, if it is, at least initially, only a designed (virtual) space, it is the "design-imagination" that is the source, running from the head through the hand to the production of the image conceived in drawing or model. In this sense, it is clear that—no matter how well-trained and eloquent the possibilities of craftsmanship and technology may be—they are of little use if spatial imagination, whether for real or virtual spaces, is not sufficiently present or cannot be formed. An architectural education that aims to be more than simply a theoretical and practical transfer of knowledge in service to the fine arts, but one with the necessary skills to become a professional architect successfully designing spaces, cannot avoid addressing this problem. Just as a fundamental musical predisposition is taken for granted in musical education—one which must be proven before assuming a course of studies—this should apply analogously to a fundamental spatial imagination and the study of architecture. Since this is unfortunately not the case, we learn our profession through everyday practice, both in the office and

2 Fernand Léger, *Trois Faces*, 1926

3 Frontispiece from Vitriuvius's *Ten Books on Architecture*, 1567

during our studies. Interestingly, it is not—as one might perhaps assume—architecture students in their first year of undergraduate study after high school who most need to develop these skills, but rather surprisingly, it is those who have completed apprenticeships as drafting technicians. Although they have the necessary knowledge to execute technically correct representations of space in their plans, it is unfortunately far from self-evident that they are also fluent in perceiving and comprehending the delineated space. Professional vocational training in (structural) drafting in particular has dedicated itself to planimetric representation, and not to the concept of space. Even though contemporary CAAD drawing methods are increasingly capable of depicting the spatial fusion of planimetrically produced parts and their spatial effects, these hyper-professional computer programs can only support information management and the technical fusion of the parts—albeit in an impressive manner. Yet they cannot compensate for a lack of spatial imagination on the part of the designer or architect. In our opinion, this is an essential prerequisite for the conception of spatial forms and sequences, which are then captured in drawings, allowing their "buildability" to be verified, step-by-step, through plans. Creating a classic set of plans, which divides the design into a large number of individual parts that can be depicted in two dimensions, can only be linked to one another by well-developed spatial imagination, allowing them to be mentally assembled into a three-dimensional whole. The two-dimensional drawing follows the three-dimensional design, and is therefore an artifact of the design process rather than its originator. In drawings, a design idea or a spatial effect can be assessed, further developed, and refined—but it cannot improve an irreplaceable sense of spatial imagination.

My years spent training third-year architecture students at the ZHAW—of which eighty percent were drafting technicians and twenty percent high-school graduates or students from other construction-related professions—allow me to state, as previously explicated, that the ability to imagine a complex spatial condition "using the mind's eye" cannot, unfortunately, be assumed as a fundamental form of basic knowledge. Even if the utilized drawing technique itself seems convincing, at least at first glance, a closer look at the plans all too often reveals that spatial transitions are not under control, or are represented incorrectly. It is difficult to say whether this results from insufficient focus on developing an understanding of spatial issues in technical drafting studies, or if such issues perhaps may not be able to be transmitted or learned. Corresponding experiences in design theory lead to the conclusion that, above all, a basic knowledge of "spatial thinking" is not easy to convey didactically. One must assume that—similar to the question of musicality—predisposition is an essential, if not decisive component of success.

Even if relatively weak basic aptitude can be gradually improved through targeted exercises and/or professional routines, training alone, without such a corresponding predisposition, does not seem to lead to success. Nevertheless, the idea of training—as this book implies is possible in the sense of a playful deepening and improvement of one's own abilities—is certainly not without impact. It is even more effective if the exercises are completed at the beginning of students' course of studies, such that initial conclusions about their aptitude or deficits in spatial perception can be

4 Giovanni Battista Piranesi, *Carceri VII*, 1760

reflected upon. I assume that self-awareness and self-evaluation on this most essential aspect of the architectural profession—made possible by this book—will be of great benefit to students. Especially at the beginning of one's studies—or better yet, in advance thereof, such as part of a pre-study internship required for high school graduates or as part of a draftsman's apprenticeship—this book could be a great asset for this course of study, since highly developed spatial imagination is a prerequisite for maturing one's own representational techniques and styles. It seems the eternal question of the chicken and the egg has been clarified: The ability to imagine spatial complexities takes precedence significantly over the ability to depict it. No matter how successful a spatial representation may be, it cannot be perceived as such without a fundamentally spatial imagination. Since spatial imagination is such a basic prerequisite for professions related to architecture, it would be highly advantageous if students could acquire it when beginning their studies—or better yet, before pursuing them—as they would have enough time to reconsider this path before continuing it for several years in vain.

URGENCY

Dieter Dietz, Lucía Jalón Oyarzun, Julien Lafontaine Carboni, and Teresa Cheung

In a time when the depletion of reason seems to have become a normality—and a fundamental disruption of the ecosystem forecasts its imminence through abnormal climate events—the question that comes to mind, first and foremost, is about the foundations of society and life as a whole. By extension, this question is one of architecture—a foundational kind of knowledge if there ever was such a thing. Under these circumstances, we can't help but wonder if the "fundamentals" that we have been taught by our teachers, by history, and by our own experience conducting our profession are adequate for the present moment. How should we learn from the incredibly rich and abundant substance amassed by the many cultures of this planet? Which values will have to be abandoned or entirely replaced, if we want to recognize this wealth and reclaim agency?

Emergence/Plurality

In our teaching and research activities, we emphasize two aspects that we deem fundamental to rethinking architecture's agency. The first is to reclaim and sustain architecture's emergent nature. We understand this notion in a deeply political way, by accepting that the outcomes of our actions as architects cannot be controlled. Architecture is a practice in motion; it does not belong to a mechanically conceived world that can be divided into a series of well-defined problems and solved by shaping objects and forms. Rather, architecture is always entangled in existence: the expression of an immanent and endless movement. Being alive—us, the environment, and our society—we all are in a perpetual state of becoming. Therein, every architectural act is the expression of a complex cultural and technical assemblage, from which the formal devices that we invent to trigger their unfolding and diversification emerge as gestures and extensions of our bodies.[1] As such, they are in a constant state of transformation. Architecture is therefore both an expression and concretization[2] of this "becoming" condition, and how we act on space must encompass this motion, learn from it, and articulate from and with it. The second aspect we consider essential is considering architecture's collective and plural nature. Architecture is never made alone—its practice always implies a collective endeavor—but it is also the assemblage of complex multiplicities, from the smallest of houses to the largest of cities. The Roman poet Lucretius wrote how *in uno tempore, tempora multa latent*: under one single moment, there are several temporalities beating together.[3] Could we speak here of something akin to a "plural spatiality," implying that, under one singular space, endless spatialities beat, ceaselessly becoming and interacting with one another? Confronted with this plural spatiality, could we consider architecture as a means of communicating, of composing a common ground interweaving the multitude of spaces—a common ground understood as medium that densifies and reorients the relational quality of the real?[4] The way architectural languages, tools, and practices manage to grasp and operate within this collective and multiple nature, but also how they are simultaneously defined and shaped by it, plays a fundamental role in how we conceive the education of an architect. Our practice exteriorizes this entanglement of dimensions,[5] while gestures—and the spatial dispositions, makings, and significations that emerge through them—form a dynamic cultural and technical fabric of matter, languages, repertoires, and strategies. This we make *together*, and making is as intrinsically linked to thinking, as is the will of the soul that allows a gesture to take place.[6]

Scaffolding/Protostructure

What kind of spatial abilities can we develop to sustain and enhance these emergent and collective dimensions? To us, the pedagogical framework is a field of experimentation, wherein fundamental research, design research, and education meet on a horizontal common ground. Theoretical concepts filter into the studio, and studio practices open up questions and problems grasped through fundamental research activities, or are further developed by design research. Such interferences between research and teaching are seen in mutual interplay in the conceptual and structural model supports and "protostructures"—as defined and

---

1   See Stiegler, Bernard. *La technique et le temps, La Philosophie en effet.* Paris: Galilée/Cité des sciences et de l'industrie, 1994.
2   Simondon, Gilbert. *L'individuation à la lumière des notions de forme et d'information.* Grenoble: Millon, 2005.
3   See verses 794–796, book IV of Lucretius's *On the nature of the universe.* Oxford: Clarendon Press, 1997.
4   Easterling, Keller. *Medium Design.* Moscow: Strelka Press, 2018.
5   See Stiegler, Bernard. *La technique et le temps, La Philosophie en effet.* Paris: Galilée/Cité des sciences et de l'industrie, 1994.
6   We refer here to Tim Ingold's critique of hylomorphism in *Making: anthropology, archaeology, art and architecture.* London/New York: Routledge, 2013.

used in our studio—which led to the development and integration of the concept of scaffolding, which in turn feeds back to the studio practice.[7]

In his article "Minds: Extended or Scaffolded," Kim Sterelny states that "human cognitive capacities both depend on and have been transformed by environmental resources. Often these resources have been preserved, built, or modified precisely because they enhance cognitive capacities. The extended mind hypothesis proposes that human cognitive systems include external components." Accordingly, the "scaffolding" theory proposes that cognitive processes are supported—scaffolded—by environmental resources. Following this logic, spatial thinking and abilities, if not supported by tools and instruments and the environment, would comprise an unbearable cognitive load. Furthermore, these external resources are considered possible driving forces to processes such as imagination, which emphasize a more active, agential, and inventive role of environment and nature than the term "resources" allows us to conceive. This input from cognitive sciences therefore encourages us to envision the studio, the program, and the human organization of our teaching activities as resources—or as a field of cognitive supports.[8]

The *protostructure*, in turn, designates the set of living and nonliving agents that allows for the extension or support of one's cognitive capacities, through the solicitation of additional and emergent resources. The value of care in this frame is emphasized: the more reliable and trustworthy a resource, the more it enhances material continuities, processes' resilience, and the potential of things to extend cognitive processes. Accordingly, the *protostructure* aims to foster the trust[9] of each individual regarding his or her own and/or their shared resources, but also encourages evolution toward individualization. The environment of the studio—its temporalities, and more broadly, space itself—are considered enablers, possessing an "agency" as actors of the process; both are then transformed into a field of emergence, in which each cognitive process can be supported in a myriad of ways. *Protostructures*, for instance, articulated as a light timber framework, can then act as catalysts between individuals for collective decision-making

and design processes. As such, when becoming a physical cognitive support for collective conception, *protostructures* are structures in a *proto-state*, ready to receive any manner of alteration in themselves.[10]

Discussing spatial abilities through the realm of *protostructure* engages our focus on spatial knowledge as a capacity to understand, follow, and act with matter in a constant flux of motion. Spatial ability is then agency; and making architecture becomes a way to relate to the world, a way in which the world will support our actions and cognitive processes—a process of imagination with and of the world.

Space/Imagination

Every action has a spatial effect, from the minor gesture to the largest interventions—they all put a new relational fabric of the real into motion. All these spatial modes, disturbances, and reorganizations challenge our imagination. But imagination, even if sustained by the outside world, remains deeply embodied. The images *(Vorstellungen)* it stages are always anchored in the materiality of our body, and cannot be paralleled, delegated, or substituted by any foreign artifact. Accordingly, concern for both matter and its link to our imagination must be at the heart of our investigations. One of the main strategies to nurture this concern is to foster drawing, its gestures and traces, as both trigger and medium of imagination. Drawing articulates endlessly rich and plural ways of thinking. In the design studio we foster drawing as a way to empower imagination towards action and critical conception—in embodied immersion as opposed to passive consumption.[11] First-year students experience this catalyzing role of drawings firsthand. The links between imagination and materiality are then expanded, spatialized, and turned into built elements, crafted by the same hands that drew them and assembled into a collective artifact. This plural and emergent dimension of the final artifact is essential. We want to encourage the contributive disposition of the architect to real situations: creating places and social situations based on a new social contract and an idea of architectures of contribution.[12] We believe that engaging with one place that concerns and matters to us makes a real difference, and that teaching and research is not only about taking critical positions; it is about enabling architectural gestures, practices, and actions that can start to parallel and interfere in the margins of the macro-scale that binds us so much today. We believe immersed, bottom-up,

7   See Clark, Andy, and David Chalmers. "The Extended Mind." In *Analysis* 58, No. 1, 7–19, January 1998. Clark, Andy. *Supersizing the Mind: Embodiment, Action, and Cognitive Extension.* Oxford: Oxford University Press USA, 2008. Most significantly, for a theoretical exploration of this notion's architectural consequences in the contemporary city, see Negueruela del Castillo, Darío. "The City of Extended Emotions." unpublished PhD dissertation, EPFL, 2017.

8   Vygotsky, Lev S. *Mind in Society: The Development of Higher Psychological Processes.* Cambridge, MA: Harvard University Press, 1980. Vygotsky, Lev S. *The Collected Works of L. S. Vygotsky: Problems of the Theory and History of Psychology.* Berlin: Springer Science & Business Media, 1997.

9   The notion of trust in relation to scaffolding is introduced into the work of Sterelny, Kim. "Minds: Extended or Scaffolded?" In *Phenomenology and the Cognitive Sciences* 9, No. 4, 465–481, December 2010. We also analyzed this aspect in relation to the HOUSE 1 protostructure in the forthcoming article by Negueruela Del Castillo, Dario et al. "Transformational Identities, Learning Scaffolding and Spatial Knowledge in Architectural Education. The Case of First Year Design Studio Teaching at EPFL." In *Charrette, Journal of Architectural Educators* 6, No. 1, 2019.

10 See Mignon, Agathe Claire Estelle. "Protostructure, Archéologie et Hypothèse d'une Architecture-Support." (unpublished PhD dissertation, EPFL, 2019).

11 See the chapter "Drawing for Real." In Dietz, Dieter, Matthias Michel, and Daniel Zamarbide (eds.), *All about Space (Vol. 3): Beyond the Object.* Zurich: Park Books, 2018.

12 See Industrialis, Ars. Économie de la contribution (n.d.) http://arsindustrialis.org/vocabulaire-economie-de-la-contribution (accessed 19 November 2019).

1 ALICE-EPFL, *House 1*, Lausanne, 2016

2 ALICE-EPFL, *House 2*, Zurich, 2017

grassroots movement must go hand in hand with rearticulating ontologies, situated both in local ecologies and in one planetary garden.[13]

We recently launched the *HOUSES* series[14] to emphasize the importance of the collective act. We hypothesized the possibility to think, design, and build one single project with 250 people, in which each participant is simultaneously author, co-author, builder, and maker. Underlining the emergent nature of architectural practice, our existential position is, by logic, one of immersion. This is articulated as a condition of "being-in": in making, and literally, in constructing the architecture that we have conceived and designed. We have pushed immersion as being-in space, as a phenomenological architecture. We have accentuated *inside-ness* as a collective phenomenon, by working in large groups and by leaving the sheltered academic environment, constructing full-scale projects in public places accessible to all. Each of the *HOUSES* that we have collectively built since 2016 is a forum; to mount these exchanges of ideas, gestures, and spaces built by many souls—to scaffold these communications—we used the aforementioned concept of *protostructure*.[15]

Landscape as Scaffolding

Yet the question of how we situate these architectures persists. The first iteration of our program *Becoming Léman* saw this very *protostructure* becoming fragmented and dissipated into multiple sites across a landscape. We need to fight against the reduction of architecture to building, and instead focus and help our students realize and be able to work with the architectural potential of materialities previously kept off grounds.[16] For this reason, we continue to explore how to relate architectures to the ground and beyond: how to situate ideas and spatial constructs—not only in society, but also in relation to our environment in its many different forms; not only as site or resource, but also as an agent deeply involved in our acting on space.

With our attention to landscape as scaffolding, we investigate these possibilities by sounding the waters and grounds of the relationship between architecture and our planetary garden.[17] To attain this common ground, as a respectful material involvement with our planet, we hope to develop architecture and its relationship to the ground simultaneously. In order to achieve that, we elaborate, test, and investigate the potential of *protofigure* and *protofiguration* as means, concepts, and tools to inscribe habitat and cultural imaginaries about our being in the world into the terrain.[18] We hope and believe that such an architectural approach can shift values—not only within our discipline, but also in broader social and cultural realms.

13 Clément, Gilles. *Le jardin planétaire*. Paris: Parc de la Villette/Albin Michel, 1999.

14 See Dietz, Dieter, Matthias Michel, and Daniel Zamarbide (eds.). *All about Space (Vol. 2): House 1 Catalogue*. Zurich: Park Books, 2018.

15 We developed this notion of space and protostructures as catalysts of imagination in Dietz, Dieter et al. "HOUSE 1 Protostructure: Enhancement of Spatial Imagination and Craftsmanship Between the Digital and the Analogical." In *Digital Wood Design (Vol 24)*, edited by Fabio Bianconi and Marco Filippucci, 1229–1252. Cham: Springer International Publishing, 2019.

16 Several authors have advanced this necessity for a long time; recently it has been Keller Easterling who developed the most lucid and coherent approach to this problem with her notion of active form in *The Action Is the Form: Victor Hugo's TED Talk* (Moscow: Strelka Press, 2012): "The designer of active forms is designing not the field in its entirety but rather the delta or the means by which the field changes—not only the shape or contour of the game piece but also a repertoire for how it plays."

17 Clément, Gilles. *Le jardin planétaire*. Paris: Parc de la Villette/Albin Michel, 1999.

18 *Protofigurations* are both an instrument of analysis and a potential tool of design. They designate two series of operations: one that is performed during a settlement or a foundation, outlining psychosocially and/or materially new geographies, and one which consists in the re-inscription of a spatial order into psychosocial bodies through embodied practices. See Lafontaine, Julien. "*Protofiguration*, opérations d'installation." In *L'archaïque et ses possibles aujourd'hui* (Paris: GERPHAU/Metis Presse 2020).

3 ALICE, *House 3*, Kanal–Centre Pompidou, Brussels, 2018

4 ALICE, *Houses*, Evian, 2019

It is in the spirit of *urgency* that we propose to engage with values other than efficiency, profitability, or the long-standing knowledge of architectural types and languages. Grounds, plants, structures, rhythms, details, materials may all evolve by themselves into new forms through the interplay with many and in continual, ongoing deliberation. To find a new spatial commons, resisting reduction to property, to demarcation lines, and to both political and architectural representation, because they are the expression of the immanent self-production of the real. What would happen if we started thinking about these commons as parallel structures that we can traverse, cut, or navigate; as fields of potentials that draw out new collective ideas, to be brought into material life through open operations, intrinsically coordinated?[19] We must think of new canvases and new tools, in order to unlearn and relearn architecture. Values will shift and form and may be very different: projects and resulting spaces will be material articulations of liminalities, and potentials articulated by material and temporal processes. And so, we go back to the beginning, back to the sense of urgency that pushes us to address these potentialities—fully aware of our incapacity to control

them, and comprehend that in order for our world (and our knowledge) to survive, it must be embodied, and thus political, ethical, ecological, and economical beyond mere capitalism.

Architecture is inherently political, not because it applies a particular ideological program, but because these two fields share a common ontological ground. The same potential of bodies establishing our being together in a political community allows us to situate ourselves and compose complex forms of spatiality.[20] Consequently, the way we operate in space reconfigures matter, places or uses, as well as communities, cultures, ecologies, imaginaries, and values: in summary, life in all its forms.[21] Thus, our intent to act upon space must be ascertained as a collective responsibility, in which we must, first and foremost, call the values that demand full control over these actions into question. Instead, we must reclaim their embodied nature and their link to these emergent phenomena. Because who or what governs life and us? What are the values that truly matter?

19 See Bühlmann, Vera. "Architectonic disposition: ichnography, scaenography, orthography." In *Posthuman Glossary*, edited by Rosi Braidotti and Maria Hlavajova. London: Bloomsbury, 2018.; and the idea of "parallelism of structure," in which a new potential appears between things, rather than within themselves only.

20 See Jalón Oyarzun, Lucía. Excepción y cuerpo rebelde: lo político como generador de una arquitectónica menor / "Exception and the rebel body: the political as generator of a minor architecture." unpublished PhD dissertation, Higher Technical School of Architecture of Madrid (UPM), 2017.

21 See Bennett, Jane. *Vibrant matter: a political ecology of things*. Durham: Duke University Press, 2010.

MEASURING SPATIAL ABILITIES

HOW TO TEST AN ARCHITECT'S SPATIAL ABILITY

Andri Gerber and Michal Berkowitz

"We, the architects, are tied to the correct understanding of our work by our fellow human beings
more than any other discipline. For it is up to
them whether or not our aspirations will blos-
som or wither. This is why we should never tire
of inviting them to the workshop of our will."
Fritz Schumacher, 1916[1]

Welcome to the "Workshop of Our Will"

As expressed in the quote by Fritz Schumacher, as architects, we should invite non-architects to the "workshop of
our will"—a wonderful metaphor that unites making and
thinking with a slightly handcrafted touch—as often as possible. According to Schumacher, we are obliged to explain
to non-architects why we are doing what we do, how we
do it, and why we think it is important, in order for them
to support us. Thus we should never tire of explaining the
unexplainable, over and over.

In order to do so—or at least to get a bit closer to communicating the "unspeakable" of space and of its design—it
is very important to uncover the means and methods we
employ to achieve a certain result. The research project
described in this book was set to investigate some of the
elements in the spatial thinking of architects. It presents
one possible means of exploring these questions.

This rather tired metaphor of the "workshop" touches one
known aspect of the profession of architecture: the frustration architects have with their lack of ability to explain
why they think something is important to a client or a family
member, or why they consider certain buildings to have
architectural qualities while others do not, and so forth.
It also expresses the frustration of architecture students
when trying to explain what they are trying to do to their
assistants and professors, only to realize that these people
see something completely different in the project. Therefore, as architects, we should invite not only non-architects,
but also architects, to our "workshop of the will" when we
think we have understood something that is not yet common knowledge, which is the case with this book. While the
idea that spatial ability is crucial for architects and architecture students may be viewed as common knowledge, this

book presents empirical evidence for this assumption, and
highlights some points beyond the realm of common knowledge (and there is still a lot of work to do in this direction!).
In light of the rich history of attempts and misunderstandings in bringing architecture and the empirical sciences together, as mentioned in the introduction to this book—some
quite productive indeed—the first rationale for the project
presented here was therefore to construct a bridge between
architecture and the cognitive sciences around the notion of
"space." It was not intended to remain a theoretical speculation, but instead, should include practical applications in
teaching and design.[2] The second rationale of the project
was to assess this *dreidimensionale Vorstellung* or *Raumsinn*—spatial ability—and find a way to measure it. Among
many possible empirical approaches, we have chosen the
psychometric approach. This included the use of existing
as well as the development of new psychometric tests.
Psychometrics—literally the measurement of the *psyche*, as
expressed in knowledge, skills, abilities, etc.—is a branch
of psychology with origins in the early study of individual
differences (e.g. Galton, Spearman, Thurstone), as well as
experimental psychology, with experiments like those conducted by Gustav Theodor Fechner on the golden ratio.[3]
There is a long tradition of using and developing psychometric tests to assess cognitive abilities, including spatial
abilities, which have been identified as an important indica-
tor for success in STEM disciplines.[4] One example, which is
constantly referred to for demonstrating the importance of
spatial ability to science, is the discovery of the structure
of DNA as a double helix by Francis Crick (1916–2004) and
James Watson (*1928). Based on images obtained by Rosa-
lind Franklin (1920–1958) and Maurice Wilkins (1916–2004),
this breakthrough required a great deal of spatial ability to

2   The metaphor of the bridge appears to be pertinent: architecture is that
    which spans between these different shores—art, sciences, but also society,
    culture, politics, techniques, and craftsmanship—and allows for the experi-
    ence of this in between space (which without a bridge would remain unat-
    tainable). Yet, we can only walk through this space of the bridge; we cannot
    really dwell on it—with a few obvious exceptions. This space can be traversed
    but not really grasped. And only architecture is capable of constructing the
    spaces that can be experienced through building projects.
3   Gerber, Andri, Tibor Joanelly, and Oya Atalay Franck. *Proportions and Cogni-
    tion in Architecture and Urban Design*. Berlin: Reimer Verlag, 2019.
4   Newcombe, Nora S. "Picture this. Increasing Math and Science Learning
    by Improving Spatial Thinking." In *American Educator*, 29–34, 2010. Uttal,
    David H., Nathaniel G. Meadow, Elizabeth Tipton, Linda L. Hand, Alison R.
    Alden, Christopher Warren, and Nora S. Newcombe. "The Malleability of
    Spatial Skills: A Meta-Analysis of Training Studies." In *Psychological Bulletin*,
    352–402, June 4, 2012. Berkowitz, Michal and Elsbeth Stern. "Which Cog-
    nitive Abilities Make the Difference? Predicting Academic Achievements in
    Advanced STEM Studies." In *Journal of Intelligence* 6, No. 4, 48, 2018.

1   Schumacher, Fritz. *Grundlagen der Baukunst. Studien zum Beruf des
    Architekten*. Munich: Verlag von Georg D. W. Callwey, 1916, p. 10.

imagine this structure in three-dimensional space. Correspondingly, there is a lot of research and literature about spatial ability in the STEM disciplines, although there is less for architecture, primarily due to the difficulties mentioned above.[5] Research thus aimed not just to uncover correlations between spatial ability and success in STEM disciplines, but it also pointed to another very important aspect: spatial ability is malleable and can be improved.[6] This implies that spatial ability is not given and unchangeable, but rather, can be enhanced through specific forms of training.

Spatial abilities are required in so many situations, in the words of Nora Newcombe: "Spatial thinking concerns the locations of objects, their shapes, their relations to each other, and the paths they take as they move. All of us think spatially in many everyday situations: when we consider rearranging the furniture in a room, when we assemble a bookcase using a diagram, or when we relate a map to the road ahead of us. We also use spatial thinking to describe non-spatial situations, such as when we talk about being close to a goal or describe someone as an insider."[7] Spatial abilities are consequently subdivided into different categories, yet there is no clear agreement regarding their exact classification, and some seem to overlap. Williams, Sutton, and Allen, for example, relied on a distinction made by P. H. Maier (1994), and differentiate between five factors of spatial ability: Spatial Relation (SR), Spatial Perception (SP), Spatial Visualization (SV), Mental Rotation (MR), and Spatial Orientation (SO).[8] Other classifications based on the psychometric approach have identified similar dimensions, with some variation in the exact classifications.[9] More recent taxonomies have been introduced by Resnick and Shipley, who distinguished between rigid and non-rigid transformations,[10] and by Uttal and his collaborators, who suggest four categories that result from cross-tabulating

the dimensions of intrinsic-extrinsic and dynamic-static.[11] Our project was influenced by the work of Thomas Shipley and colleagues, who developed spatial ability tasks for geology students, designed to capture their specific spatial abilities.[12]

The research project lasted for three years, from 2016 to 2019, and was built on three steps: the first was to use existing tests for spatial ability to create a baseline; the second was to develop a new test specifically adapted to the spatial ability of architects; and the third was to improve the newly developed test and track for possible changes in performance after students gained more experience through their architectural education. The tests were administered to architecture students from several Swiss architectural schools and a few students from Northumbria University (UK) and Technion (ISR). One of the most challenging tasks was actually to motivate architectural students to participate in our testing sessions, as they are not used to participating in experiments, and because their studies are very time-intensive. Thus, we were confronted with relatively little interest from students and needed to motivate them to participate.

In the first round, we administered the following existing tests: the Mental Rotation Test (MRT) (Peters, Laeng, Latham, Jackson, Zaiyouna, and Richardson, 1995), PVST Rotations (Guay, 1977), The Paper Folding Test (Eckstrom, French, Harman, and Derman, 1976), The Mental Cutting Test (MCT) (CEEB, 1939), and Spatial Orientation Test (Kozhevnikov and Hegarty, 2001). Two subtests—Figural Matrices and Number Series from an intelligence test battery (Intelligenz-Struktur-Test (I-S-T) 2000R)—were included as general ability measures. We administered these tests to 186 architecture students from five different schools in Switzerland (ZHAW, ETHZ, EPFL, HSLU, and FHNW). Most of the spatial tests appeared to be too easy for our sample, with scores approaching a ceiling effect. The two tests that showed enough variability were the MRT and MCT. Of these, the MCT seemed most relevant to architects, as master's students outperformed bachelor's students on this test, but not on the MRT. Given the fact that drawing cross-sections is a central part of architectural design and education, the result was not surprising, and provided some indications about the direction we should take with our new tests. In the second phase, we only tested students from three schools of architecture (ZHAW, ETH, and EPFL). In this phase, we administered two existing spatial ability tests (Mental Rotation Test and Mental Cutting Test), one general reasoning test (Figural Matrices), and three newly developed

5   Ji Cho, Young. "Spatial ability, creativity, and studio performance in architectural design." In T. Fischer, K. De Biswas, J.J. Ham, R. Naka, W.X. Huang, *Beyond Codes and Pixels: Proceedings of the 17th International Conference on Computer-Aided Architectural Design Research in Asia.* Association for Computer-Aided Architectural Design Research in Asia (CAADRIA), Hong Kong, 131–140, 2012. Sutton, K., and A. Williams. "Implications of Spatial Abilities on Design Thinking." In *Conference Proceedings. Design & Complexity: Design Research Society International Conference,* Montreal, 131–140, 2012.

6   Newcombe, Nora S. "Picture this. Increasing Math and Science Learning by Improving Spatial Thinking." In *American Educator,* 29–34, Summer 2010. Uttal, David, Nathaniel G. Meadow, Elizabeth Tipton, Lind L. Hand, Alison R. Alden, and Christopher Warren. "The Malleability of Spatial Skills: A Meta-Analysis of Training Studies." In *Psychological Bulletin* 139, No. 2, 352–402, 2013.

7   Newcombe, Nora S. "Picture this" (2010), p. 31.

8   Williams, A, K. Sutton, and R. Allen. "Spatial Ability: Issues associated with engineering and gender." In *19th Annual Conference of the Australasian Association for Engineering Education: To Industry and Beyond; Proceedings of the Institution of Engineers,* Australia, 228, 2008. Maier, P.H. *Räumliches Vorstellungsvermögen: Komponenten, geschlechtsspezifische Differenzen, Relevanz, Entwicklung und Realisierung in der Realschule.* Berlin: Peter Lang, 1994.

9   Carroll, John B. *Human Cognitive Abilities: A survey of factor-analytic studies.* Oxford: Cambridge University Press, 1993.

10 Resnick, Ilyse, and Thomas F. Shipley. "Breaking new ground in the mind: an initial study of mental brittle transformation and mental rigid rotation in science experts." In *Cognitive processing* 14, No. 2, 143–152, 2013.

11 Uttal, David H., David I. Miller, and Nora S. Newcombe. "Exploring and enhancing spatial thinking: Links to achievement in science, technology, engineering, and mathematics?" In *Current Directions in Psychological Science* 22, No. 5, 367–373, 2013.

12 Shipley, Thomas F., Basil Tikoff, Carol Ormand, and Cathy Manduca. "Structural Geology Practice and Learning, from the Perspective of Cognitive Science." In *Journal of Structural Geology* 54, 72–84, September 2013.

1 Peters, Laeng, Latham, Jackson, Zaiyouna, and Richardson, *Mental Rotation Test,* 1995

tests: the Urban Layout Test, Indoor Perspective Test, and Packing Test. We had developed an additional test—the Mental Construction Test—but due to time limitations, it was not used in our testing sessions.[13] An adaptation of it is included in the training material in this book.

In this iteration, we had a total of 593 students participating: 502 bachelor's and 91 master's students. Master's students outperformed bachelor's students on all of the new tests, as well as on the Mental Cutting Test. On the Urban Layout Test this advantage was more consistent for one set of view points, presumably those that were solved first in each item. All the new tests correlated significantly with the existing spatial ability tests, confirming that they measure spatial ability in a broader sense. However, the data did not indicate a stronger correlation among the new tests when compared to their correlation with existing tests. Thus, we could not confirm a specific "architectural" spatial ability based on inter-test correlations.

Based on the results of this second round, we attempted to improve the individual items of the new tests, and then administered them again to students from the three schools—including retesting 138 students from the second phase. We also administered the test to a cohort of students from the Technical University of Kaiserslautern. The test results improved overall, and some of the findings of Phase 1 were confirmed: the new tests correlated with existing spatial ability tests, but no clear differentiation emerged for the new tests as measuring a common ability that differed from existing tests. Additionally, performance on some of the tests improved in the second iteration, hence, after gaining more experience with architecture. The improved performance was noted on one of the new tests (Packing), as well as on both existing tests (MCT and MRT). In this phase, the majority of students were in their second year of their bachelor studies, whereas a very small group of master's students participated. Therefore, we could not verify whether master's students still outperform beginners one year later. The weaker than expected overlap among the newly developed tests could be explained by the fact that our new test items were quite heterogeneous, possibly with too much variability across stimuli. At the same time, this could also indicate that such differences are too subtle, too strongly bound with the more general spatial skills captured by existing tests—or that these are not yet developed at this relatively early stage in an architectural career. In this regard, we welcome further work on our new tests, not only in the field of architecture but also in other disciplines. Furthermore, we only had a chance to compare architecture with biology students in the first phase of the project, through the existing tests. This revealed no differences between the groups on most of the tests, with the exception of the Mental Cutting Test, in which architecture students outperformed biology students. Thus, it would be interesting for future research to follow students from these different disciplines into later points in their studies, and compare their performance on specialized tests such as those developed here. If the specialized tests indeed capture processes that are more relevant to architecture, we would expect more pronounced differences on these tests between architects and non-architects.

One important aspect of our research was gender difference; this has been consistently documented in previous research, in particular, in mental rotation tasks. In our three steps, men outperformed women in all spatial ability tests, although men and women did not differ in their general reasoning ability. These findings can be explained by various factors, some directly related to the spatial content e.g. slower spatial visualization among women, or to solving strategies, whereas others may have to do with situational factors, such as the setting of group testing and the time limitation. The causes for differences in spatial performance among men and women are multiple, and have been extensively discussed.[14] These include, for example, differences in prior experiences with spatial tasks, with boys engaging more often in activities that foster spatial thinking than girls. In light of the very problematic gender gap in architecture, which is primarily culturally determined—a lack of role models, incompatibility with part-time work, and a highly competitive environment—this difference in spatial ability might imply an additional obstacle for women in the profession. Interestingly, compared to differences at

13 The test was actually only used in one testing session. The choice not to use it was also pragmatic: as architecture students were only willing to take a shorter test, we had to eliminate something.

14 Levine, Susan C., Alana Foley, Stella Lourenco, Stacy Ehrlich, and Kristin Ratliff. "Sex differences in spatial cognition: Advancing the conversation." In *Wiley Interdisciplinary Reviews: Cognitive Science* 7, No. 2, 127–155, March/ April 2016.

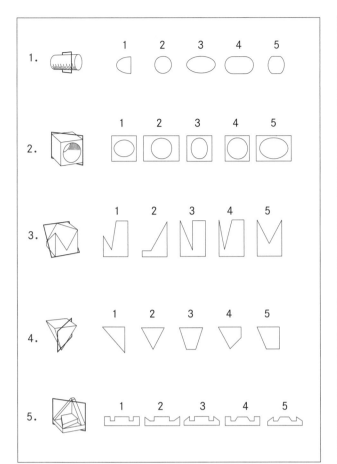

2 CEEB, *Mental Cutting Test,* 1939

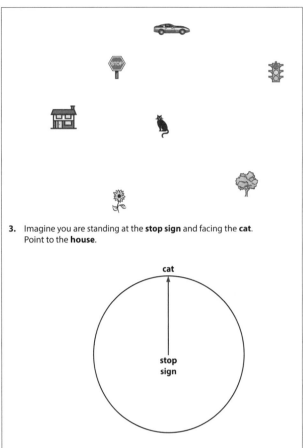

3. Imagine you are standing at the **stop sign** and facing the **cat**. Point to the **house**.

3 Kozhevnikov, Hegarty, *Spatial Orientation Test,* 2001

the bachelor level, the gap seemed smaller at the master level, which may indicate a proportionally higher increase in spatial ability during architecture studies among women relative to men. At the same time, our data showed that, after one year of architecture studies at the bachelor level, both men and women improved their spatial abilities to a similar extent. Thus, the project revealed how architectural education fosters the development of spatial abilities in both genders.

Constructing the New Tests

Developing psychometric tests is not an easy task, and a test itself, once developed, requires repeated verifications and adjustments. Psychometric tests of spatial ability, such as the Mental Rotation Test (Vandenberg and Kuse, 1978), were designed as general measures of spatial ability—namely, not bound to skills in a specific discipline. This is in order to minimize dependency on prior knowledge, so that test problems can be solved by novices too. It is for this reason that these tests are constructed in a de-contextualized, abstract manner.

While it is commonly assumed that advanced students develop expertise on specific forms of spatial ability, few

tests have been developed that capture this advanced form of spatial ability. In the case of our tests, we attempted to create decontextualized tests that would not require any prior knowledge of architectural codes—plans, sections, or technical perspectives—but would still be adapted to architecture. If successful when doing the tests, architects should outperform non-architects, and advanced students should outperform beginners.

In order to adapt the tests to architecture, specific aspects of the design process that rely on spatial abilities were isolated and transformed into test items. This required a lot of trial and error before we identified satisfying solutions. The design process has been defined in the past as an "ill-structured problem"[15] or "wicked problem"[16] because of its complexity. During this process, architects perform several steps, which are often joined in the attempt to translate an idea—a concept, through an understanding of the site and its genius loci—into a building that fulfills all technical and legal constraints. They require several instruments for this process—from drawing to diagram, from physical to 3D

---

15 Reitman, W. R. "Heuristic Decision Procedures, Open Constraints, and the Structure of Ill-Defined Problems." In M.W. Shelly and G. L. Bryan (eds.), *Human Judgements and Optimality,* New York, NY: John Wiley and Sons, 1964.

16 Rittel, Horst W. J. *Planen—Entwerfen—Design. Ausgewählte Schriften zu Theorie und Methodik.* Stuttgart: Kohlhammer, 1992.

models—and switch between different scales and perspectives, from the large urban scale to the very small scale of construction details. Thus, perspective shifts from an allocentric perspective—the birds-eye view—to the egocentric perspective, once ironically defined as the "mole-view."[17] The distinction between these two perspectives has already been theorized in the context of psychometric tests.[18] The movement from one scale to the other, and from one perspective to the other is not linear; rather, it is circular and irregular and as such cannot be broken down to one single, identifiable condition, but instead is in a constant state of flux. Here, one main problem with conventional psychometric tests is that they are designed to measure a specific type of spatial ability, and preferably, as few mental processes as possible. As soon as multiple abilities and processes are involved in a test, it is more difficult to single them out in the results. As such, one flaw of using psychometric tests in architecture is that they artificially reduce the complexity of the design to a simplified model. At the same time, this is the main advantage of such tools in comparison to other more "messy" methods. Assuming one keeps the problem of reductionism in mind, one can rely on its results. Indeed, some of our test items—in particular, the Indoor Perspective Test—were not as "pure" in isolating single spatial mental processes as items on standard tests may be. As previously mentioned, this might be one of the reasons our tests did not work exactly the way we expected. With this in mind, we designed the four new tests: the Urban Layout Test, the Indoor Perspective Test, the Packing Test, and the Mental Construction Test.

A particularly important aspect in this process of constructing a test is that—no less than carefully designing the correct answer—attention should be given to anticipating and designing possible mistakes. In order to make answer choices systematic, specific features of wrong answers were defined and manipulated across items. These features were, for example, the number of elements presented; the angles or degree of complexity; or the type of mistake they reflected. Another important lesson was that the tests had to be designed in such a way as to minimize the use of analytical and cue-based strategies. We realized that many of the tests we developed at the beginning could be solved without spatial ability, and instead, just with analytical processes of identifying cues. Subjects could look for the position of certain items or for their number and solve a test accordingly with only this information. Thus, a lot of energy was put into the development of tests that would

4 Berkowitz, Gerber, *Urban Layout Test,* Axonometry, 2019

minimize this problem and force the subjects to use their spatial imagination to solve them.

1. Urban Layout Test

In this test, a collection of shapes is presented that simulates an urban setting. The subject is asked to recognize two positions inside this setting based on four given views. The subject is thus asked to switch from an allocentric perspective of the whole urban-like layout, which is displayed from top view, to an egocentric perspective from a vantage point inside this layout. There are two options, not one, as the latter would allow for a simpler procedure of excluding the wrong answers, while the two options force the subject to mentally delve into the layout. In the test, we alternated between two variations: one in which the target layout is presented in plan, and one in which it is presented as an axonometric. The assumption was that the former would involve a greater mental load. A total of 11 different shapes—from simple to complex—were created, and these were always displayed in pairs for a total of 6 or 8 items composing the layout. Questions with more complex shapes and a larger number of shapes were more dif-

17 Gerber, Andri. "Adler oder Maulwurf? Der Städtebau und die Maßstabsfrage." In V.M. Lampugnani and R. Schützeichel (eds.) *Die Stadt als Raumentwurf: Theorien und Projekte im Städtebau seit dem Ende des 19. Jahrhunderts,* 161–179. Berlin and Munich: Deutscher Kunstverlag, 2018.
18 Kozhevnikov, Maria, David W. Schloerb, Olesay Blazhenkova, Samuel Koo, Nadeem Karimbux, R. Bruch Donoff, and Jairo Salcedo. "Egocentric versus allocentric spatial ability in dentistry and haptic virtual reality training." In *Applied Cognitive Psychology* 27, No. 3, 373–383, March 2013.

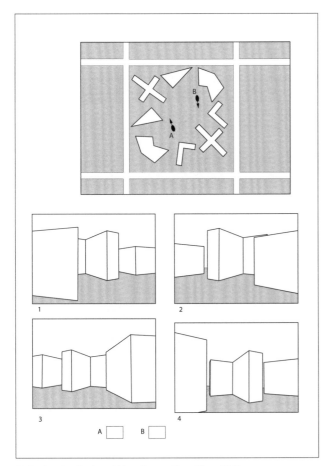

5 Berkowitz, Gerber, *Urban Layout Test,* Plan, 2019

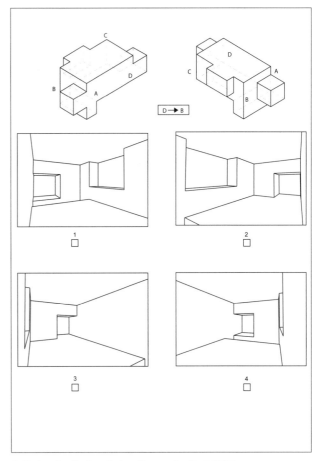

6 Berkowitz, Gerber, *Indoor Perspective Test,* 2019

ficult to solve. Furthermore, two possible general positions of the viewer were defined: one inside and one outside the array of objects. Based on this set of objects and viewers' position, we developed a series of items, in which the viewer had to choose from four very similar perspectives. Thus, the disposition was always done in accordance with the wished views and depending on their similarity. Objects in the background thus became crucial to identifying the correct answer. The main challenge was to align the objects in relation to each other and in relation to the position of the viewer. The "distractors" are therefore based on two variables: the viewer positions and the position of the objects. All perspectives are "correct," but only two correspond to the two positions.

2. Indoor Perspective Test

While the Urban Layout Test simulates an urban environment, the Indoor Test simulates the interior of a volume that could be a building. As in the previous case, the subject has to perform a change of perspective from an allocentric vision of the outside of a volume—displayed in two different angles, to allow for hidden details to be recognized—to an egocentric perspective inside it. In relation to the Urban Layout Test, the change of scale from one to the other is increased, as the target and the four possible solutions differ more strongly in size. The four options correspond to the four corners of the volume, always looking at the opposite corner, as indicated by a small caption. The distractors are correct views taken from other positions within the object. The views varied by the type of modification applied to an initial cuboid—parts of the cuboid had either been "pushed" in or out. These modifications are either perpendicular or diagonal. The volumes are thus modified in a way to create views that are similar but invert the position of these modifications. The primary mistakes of the subjects are based on an inversion of right/left or top/down.

3. Packing Test

In this test, the subject is asked to compose or deconstruct three-dimensional volumes. We assume this process is particularly relevant for architects, when designing buildings or urban settings by adding or subtracting smaller or larger volumes. There are existing psychometric tests based on a similar principle—puzzle pieces that have to be fitted

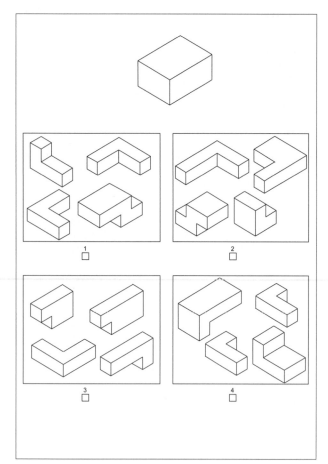

7 Berkowitz, Gerber, *Packing Test Whole to Part,* 2019

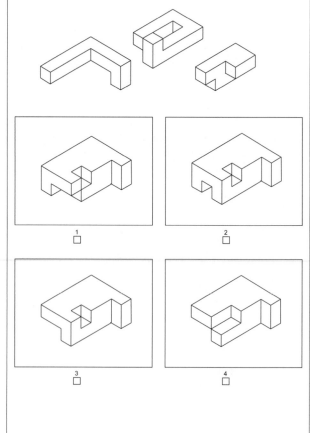

8 Berkowitz, Gerber, *Packing Test Part to Whole,* 2019

together—yet to our knowledge, none of these are three-dimensional, with exception of the Experimental Blocks Test (circa 1950).[19]

There are two variations of this new test: the target is either a whole volume—a cuboid or a cylinder—or it is a collection of object parts. In the first case, one has to identify which sets of object parts match the target exactly when put together. In the second case, one has to identify which volume is the result of putting together the given object parts. Object parts only need to be mentally moved, but not rotated. There are either three or four parts of the volume. In a pre-test phase, we discovered that questions with only two object parts were too easy, whereas more than four parts were too difficult and created a too high cognitive load. The increase of complexity is determined by the shape of the volumes with a maximum of two 90° bends per object. The distractors were always of three types for each item: (a) either the combined parts do not fill the target, (b) the combined parts fill the target but overlap, or (c) they exceed the target volume. As such, it is possible here, too, to clearly identify the types of mistakes.

4. Mental Construction Test

Similar to the Packing Test, here, items have to be added to one another. However, the focus lies in a set of instructions that are given and through which the subject has to mentally construct a target that is not provided in advance. Four options for the target are displayed, only one of which is correct. Originally, the instructions were given verbally, yet this would have made verbal skills an influencing factor and thus potentially conflate it with spatial ability. It has also been reported that many students in the arts have forms of dyslexia,[20] thus we decided to change the instructions to simple formulas. This step was also done in order to minimize confusion, and thus additional mental load, that could come from needing to translate verbal information into spatial configurations.

Starting from a simple cuboid, transformations of this cuboid are formulated—adding further cuboids, stacking them and turning them—and the subject has to choose from four possible options. Distractors comprised the number of transformations and the complexity of the transformed volumes. Mistakes are generally based on inversions, mis-

---

19 For a thorough overview of different spatial ability tests, even if outdated, see also: Eliot, John, and Ian Macfarlane Smith. *An International Directory of Spatial Tests.* Windsor: Nfer-Nelson, 1983.

20 Wolff, Ulrika, and Ingvar Lundberg. "The Prevalence of Dyslexia Among Art Students." In *Dyslexia* 8, 34–42, January 2002.

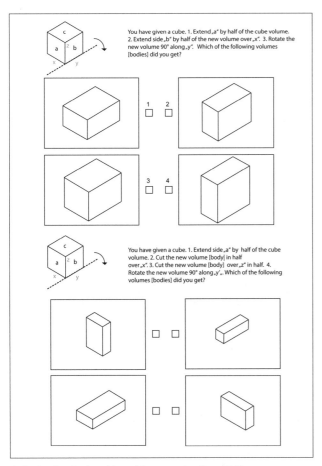

You have given a cube. 1. Extend „a" by half of the cube volume. 2. Extend side „b" by half of the new volume over „x". 3. Rotate the new volume 90° along „y". Which of the following volumes [bodies] did you get?

1 2

3 4

You have given a cube. 1. Extend side „a" by half of the cube volume. 2. Cut the new volume [body] in half over „x". 3. Cut the new volume [body] over „z" in half. 4. Rotate the new volume 90° along „y'". Which of the following volumes [bodies] did you get?

9 Berkowitz, Gerber, *Mental Construction Test,* 2019

taken transformations, and too many steps one cannot mentally reconstruct. Therefore, only a limited number of transformations are given, as otherwise the mental load becomes too high. This test was only used in one study, as we had to economize the time required to complete all the tests.[21]

21 Anyone interested can request our test by contacting either Andri Gerber at ZHAW or Michal Berkowitz at ETH Zurich.

FOSTERING SPATIAL ABILITIES WITH ARCHITECTURAL GEOMETRY

Cornelie Leopold

Spatial abilities are essential requirements for architecture, and all fields in which spatial objects and 3D reality are supposed to be created, designed, and changed. But how can these "spatial imagination" abilities and thinking in 3D be developed and improved? It thus remains an aim for architectural design education to provide suitable approaches. Architectural geometry, traditionally known as descriptive geometry, provides a chance to foster spatial abilities.

Spatial Abilities for Architectural Designing

Perception of space and our surroundings mark our starting point. Tools, like drawing and 3D modeling have the function of making the imaginations of a designer perceptible. A prerequisite for architecture is an ability to imagine space, and also to relate it to a subject like its viewer or user. In the context of perception, geometry is responsible for relating things to criteria of perception and creation. The ability to imagine spatial effects and relationships with the help of 2D drawings, images, and diagrams remains important even while working with 3D modeling programs. Geometry provides the background for creating forms, structures, and spaces that suggest spatial concepts. On the other hand, the geometry of projection and visualization helps to determine various concepts of representation and visual communication. The discipline of descriptive geometry was developed as a new and central part of engineering education in the eighteenth century, in particular by Gaspard Monge (1746–1818) at the newly founded École *Polytechnique* in France, as well as in other countries with the emerging technical universities of the nineteenth century. The subject of descriptive geometry was tasked with the representation of technical and architectural objects in the design process, formulating and learning a common language for engineers, artists, craftsmen, and workers. Monge described the role of descriptive geometry as:

"This art (Descriptive Geometry) has two principal objects. The first is to represent with exactness, from drawings which have only two dimensions, objects which have three (…). From this point of view, it is a language necessary to the man of genius when

he conceives a project, to those who are responsible for its execution, and lastly, to the artists who themselves must execute the different parts. The second objective of Descriptive Geometry is to deduce, from the exact description of bodies, all that necessarily results from their forms and their respective positions. (…) It is necessary to include it as a part of the nationwide plan for education."[1]

Later on, descriptive geometry was often seen as the discipline for teaching graphical techniques, which led to the opinion that it was obsolete in the time of digital tools like CAD programs. To avoid such a historical misunderstanding, we shall instead refer to the discipline as architectural geometry today, which also serves to focus on the two necessary tasks for such a discipline: geometric modeling and representational facilities.

As a first task, for students to get started with spatial imagination, it turned out to be a useful approach translating from 2D to 3D, and then again back to 2D. These processes in the interplay of 2D and 3D can be applied in various media: sketching, hand drawing in orthographic views, axonometrics and perspectives, digital 3D modeling, physical modeling, as well as view settings related to the digital and physical 3D models. Switching between the different representations of spatial objects and the objects themselves—as an interplay between them—is most effective in developing spatial abilities.

We took the outline of House Visser (1956) in Bergeijk, the Netherlands, designed by Gerrit Rietveld (1888–1964) and later redesigned and supplemented by Aldo van Eyck (1918–1999), as depicted by Figure 1. In a first step, the students had to look for 2D figures in the outline, which served as the basis for an abstracted building structure. These 2D figures were then further developed as 3D objects, which could be seen as the geometric abstraction of a building composition.

---

1   Monge, Gaspard. *Géométrie Descriptive.* Paris: Baudouin, 1798. https://gallica.bnf.fr/ark:/12148/bpt6k5783452x, (accessed 26 August 2019, Translated by the author), p. 2.

1 Outline and resulting 3D compositions as paper models, hand drawings or orthographic views, and axonometric drawing by student Jonny Klein, 2018

Spatial Ability Tests and Results

We conducted a series of spatial ability tests with our students of architecture and civil engineering between 1994 and 2013. The number of tested students in each year was quite high, always between 100 and 250. We used various internationally recognized tests, including the Mental Rotation Test (MRT), the Mental Cutting Test (MCT), and the Differential Aptitude Test: Space Relations (DAT).

In some years we also made comparisons with students in urban and environmental planning, mathematics, mechanical engineering, as well as industrial engineering at the Technical University Kaiserslautern. One result was that there was always a significant gender difference, with higher results for men. But there was also another result: that the gender difference in the test results was lower in study programs with smaller percentages of women. This means that women with well-developed spatial abilities had been more likely to choose these "hard" engineering study programs. In some years, we also conducted post-tests at the end of the semester, in order to look for changes in our program. We recorded the following results:

- women increased their abilities much more in the post-tests than men who had started at a low level in the pre-test;
- gender differences decreased;
- students in architecture and civil engineering increased much more in the post-test than those in mechanical engineering.

Students in architecture and civil engineering attend the descriptive geometry course, in which spatial abilities are specifically promoted, whereas students of mechanical engineering attend a reduced version of the program in the course technical drawing.

International studies have shown similar results. Kenjiro Suzuki from Japan used pre-tests and post-tests to analyze the spatial abilities of students in different teaching programs: descriptive geometry, computer graphics, engineering graphics, 3D computer-aided design, and a control group without any such courses.[2] This research showed that those courses with hand-drawn and geometric content played an important role in the enhancement of spatial abilities. Similar results were also found in numerous studies by Sheryl Sorby from the United States. Descriptive geometry courses had been mostly substituted for CAD courses in the U.S., which resulted in students having weaker spatial skills.[3] Sorby developed a course for training spatial skills, in which sketching and drawing supported by multimedia software comprised the essential elements. The course members showed significant increases in the post-tests and in the retention rates compared to the control group. Those in computer graphics courses had no significant impact in visualization skills. These international studies as well as personal experiences showed the importance of a vivid graphic spatial geometry for the development of spatial abilities.

Architectural Geometry Program to Foster Spatial Abilities

Over many years of teaching architectural geometry to students of architecture, it became obvious that many students often begin university with low levels of spatial abilities, as well as large differences in the level of their spatial abilities within the same course. We evaluated our

2   Suzuki, Kenjiro. "Activities of the Japan Society for Graphic Science—Research and Education." In *Journal for Geometry and Graphics* 6, No. 2, 225, 2002.

3   Sorby, Sheryl. "Impact of Changes in Course Methodologies on Improving Spatial Skills." In *Journal for Geometry and Graphics* 9, No. 1, 99–105, 2005.

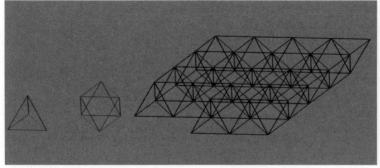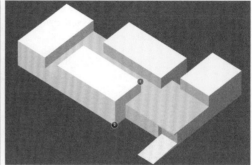

2 Examples of digital 3D models in Sketchfab®: animated 3D model of a spatial framework as tetrahedra-octahedra-packing (A. 6.10); preset of two views, top view and front view, in the 3D model of a house based on the Kirchnermuseum (1992) in Davos, by Annette Gigon and Mike Guyer (B. 4.3)

geometry program and asked the students about their experiences and assessment of our teaching program using a questionnaire.[4] Drawing examples and models were evaluated as the most helpful in supporting spatial abilities. Besides physical models, we also introduced digital 3D models accompanying the drawing examples and methods in order to suggest, in each case, spatial thinking. The platform Sketchfab® had been used for publishing and sharing the 3D models and animations. With it, the models can be used in a browser, independent from a program, and are also available in an application for smartphones and tablets. As such, most of the examples in our course script[5] and book of exercises are available as supporting digital 3D models. The two examples in Figure 2 can be inspected interactively, and in order to understand different perspectives, preset views can be chosen in several examples or processes and methods can be experienced through animations.[6]

Spatial abilities are encouraged by combining various media. In their first year of study, the students work on a small architectural design project supervised by the subjects: methods of design by Prof. Dirk Bayer and building construction by Prof. Stephan Birk. We support this first individual project to help students become aware of different views of the designed house in its surroundings, as well as relating exterior and interior views. Such perspectives, in hand-drawn geometric constructions and visualizations, are helpful to anticipate the further impact of the design, as shown in Figures 3 and 4.

These studies are important steps to understanding the parameters and the consequences for the constructed image. In order to combine this representation with the conditions of perception, light and shadow are taken into account in the perspective representations and adapted to realistic sun positions. The test tasks in this book, such as the Urban Layout and Indoor Perspective Test, correspond with the perspectival scenes of an architectural project.

Drawing while thinking three-dimensionally is an important step for developing spatial abilities. Bringing the students to a spatial understanding of all two-dimensional drawings is sometimes a long road. But knowing the geometric background of the projection methods from 3D to 2D as well as the role of the representational parameters helps to improve these skills, and therefore facilitates architectural design competencies.

---

4 Leopold, Cornelie. "Principles of a Geometry Program for Architecture–Experiences, Examples, and Evaluations." In *Journal for Geometry and Graphics* 7, No. 1, 101–110, 2003.
5 Leopold, Cornelie. *Geometrische Grundlagen der Architekturdarstellung. Mit 3D-Modellen und Animationen zur räumlichen Vorstellung.* Wiesbaden: Springer Verlag, 2019.
6 Leopold, Cornelie, Falk Ahlhelm, and Viyaleta Zhurava. "Model Collections on Sketchfab®." (accessed 26 August 2019).
   A. https://sketchfab.com/cornelieleopold/collections
   B. https://sketchfab.com/DarstellendeGeometrie/collections

3 Exterior and interior perspectives of Movie Character House
architectural project by first year student Philipp Hell, 2012

4 Interior and exterior perspectives of Hang-Glider House
architectural project by first year student Natascha Reinhardt, 2019

EXPERTISE AND THE MEANING OF SPATIAL TESTING

David Uttal

The chapters in this volume present a very well-researched and validated psychometric assessment of spatial thinking in architects. It is, to my knowledge, one of the very few tests that has been specifically designed to assess individual differences in a form of expert spatial thinking. Almost all other spatial tests are designed to assess more general spatial thinking that, in theory, is not tied to expertise in a domain or content area. For example, tests of mental rotation usually require that the test-taker imagine transformations of meaningless figures, such as cubes that have been arranged into different figures.

The authors have taken on a very challenging task: Both to map out what kinds of spatial expertise architects need to have, and to provide a psychometric assessment of these abilities. Their work can help us to think about the nature of spatial expertise. Specifically, the new test and associated research shed light on the nature of spatial expertise and on the relationship between spatial thinking and achievement in science and art fields.

The Nature of Spatial Expertise

The test and subsequent validation indicate that spatial expertise in architecture is a combination of domain content knowledge and basic spatial skills. For example, architects become very familiar with how buildings are constructed and can use elements of this expertise when solving spatial problems. In this regard, the results presented in this book highlight the important ways in which expertise affects cognition, learning, and performance. Expertise affects what we attend to, what we care about, and how we think.[1] The influences and expertise have been documented across a very wide set of domains, ranging from chess[2] to chick sexing.[3] Two examples from prior work highlight the importance of expertise in spatially rich domains.

Expert Spatial Thinking in Geology

The first example concerns the spatial cognition of expert geologists. Resnick and Shipley (2013) observed that geologists often need to think about spatial transformations that differ fundamentally from those that are assessed in typical spatial ability tests.[4] Expert geologists must understand spatial transformations that involve, for example, brittle materials that can break when subjected to forces. Non-rigid transformations have, to my knowledge, never been part of research in traditional psychometric research in spatial thinking. For example, all mental rotation studies have assumed that the figures stay together and do not change during rotation. Thus, expert spatial thinking in geologists highlights the limits of our current thinking about spatial cognition, and we can expand research to address these questions.

Shipley and colleagues demonstrated that expert geologists, but not expert chemists, can mentally transform brittle spatial configurations.[5] Figure 1 shows an example where a "faulted word," in this case, the word "eat" has been placed on a hypothetical geological fault. When the fault moves, the rock layer on which the words are written will shear and break. To read the faulted words, a person needs to think how this brittle transformation would alter the appearance of the letters.

The expert geologists could read the faulted words, even after the insertion of additional characters (e.g. questions marks) that made recognition much more difficult. In contrast, despite their generally high levels of basic spatial abilities, expert chemists could not read the faulted words. These results suggest a unique effect of geological expertise on the perception and transformation of spatial information: The expert geologists interpreted the transformation as "faulting" and transformed the information accordingly. These results reveal an entirely new skill, thinking about brittle transformations, that is not present in novices or even in expert chemists. Without expert studies, we would not realize that different forms or foci of expertise can be fundamentally different from what is usually assessed in standard spatial ability tests.

1   Chi, M. T., R. Glaser, and M. J. Farr. *The nature of expertise*. Milton Park, UK: Psychology Press, 2014.
2   Gobet, F., and N. Charness. "Expertise in chess." In K. A. Ericsson, N. Charness, P. J. Feltovich, and R. R. Hoffman (eds.), *The Cambridge handbook of expertise and expert performance*, 523–538. Cambridge, UK: Cambridge University Press, 2006.
3   Biederman, I., and M. M. Shiffrar. "Sexing day-old chicks: A case study and expert systems analysis of a difficult perceptual-learning task." In *Journal of Experimental Psychology: Learning, memory, and cognition*, 13(4), 640–645,1987.
4   Resnick, I., and T. F. Shipley. "Breaking new ground in the mind: an initial study of mental brittle transformation and mental rigid rotation in science experts." In *Cognitive processing, 14*(2), 143–152, 2013.
5   Atit, K., T. F. Shipley, and B. Tikoff. "Twisting space: Are rigid and non-rigid mental transformations separate spatial skills?" In *Cognitive processing, 14(2)*, 163–173, 2013.

Before Fragmentation
(faulting):

After Fragmentation
(faulting):

 ⇒

Before Fragmentation
(faulting):

After Fragmentation
(faulting):

e?a?t ⇒ e?ᴄ?ᴛ

1 Example of Faulted Words from Resnick and Shipley, 2013

Expert Spatial Thinking in Chemistry

Although chemists could not read the faulted words, they nevertheless possess their own forms of expertise. M. Stieff asked expert and novice chemists to rotate the traditional Shepard and Metzler figures, as well as different representations of molecules.[6] For the standard Shepard and Metzler materials, expert and novice chemists performed about the same, and the graphs indicate the traditional strong and positive relationship between angle of disparity of the stimulus and target and reaction time. However, the results were very different when chemists were asked to make judgments about representations of chemical molecules. Particularly for symmetric molecules, expert chemists were typically very fast and accurate. Most importantly, the degree of rotation did not affect their judgment; regardless of the degree of rotation, chemistry experts could make the decision as to whether the transformed figure was a rotated or reflected version of the original molecule very quickly and accurately. The chemists had learned about the chirality (or handedness) of the molecules. This spatial property is a critical aspect of many molecules and thus part of the basic knowledge of the experts. This knowledge could then be applied to the mental rotation task, allowing the experts to make the decision as to whether the molecules were rotated both quickly and accurately. There was no need to go through the challenging task of mental rotation, as they already knew whether the target molecule was a mirror image of the original.

Why are Spatial Thinking and Accomplishments in Science and the Arts Correlated?

The demonstrations of the importance of expertise in spatial thinking also shed new light on the relationship between spatial skills and accomplishments in STEM (Science, Technology, Engineering, and Mathematics) and the arts. It is well-known that performance on spatial tests correlates with achievement in science, mathematics, engineering, technology, and some art fields.[7] But why? Why are spatial ability and performance in STEM disciplines correlated? To many, the answer to this question will seem obvious: STEM and art are inherently spatial in nature, and thus, high levels of spatial ability are needed to succeed. For example, a structural geologist needs to imagine the forces that created a mountain, and an architect must imagine different perspectives as they design a structure within the constraints of the available space.

However, work on expertise in spatial thinking should lead us to consider other possible causes of the correlations between spatial ability and achievement in STEM and art-related fields. As noted elsewhere, the correlation between spatial ability and STEM achievement actually seems to decrease as the level of expertise increases. We have theorized that as performance becomes increasingly dependent on the kinds of spatial expertise discussed above, basic spatial abilities (such as the mental rotation of abstract features) actually becomes less important.[8] On this view, the correlations between spatial ability and level of achievement reflect selection factors that happened earlier in the careers of the artists, engineers, and scientists. The experts retain high levels of spatial ability, but they often rely on domain-specific knowledge when performing demanding tasks.

In summary, expert performance in spatially rich domain is fundamentally different from the performance of novices who have been the subject of almost all research thus far. However, in the last decade, researchers have begun to understand the nature of spatial expertise in several domains, and the chapters in this volume represent a very important contribution to this mission.

6 Stieff, M. "Mental rotation and diagrammatic reasoning in science." In *Learning and Instruction, 17 (2)*, 219, 2007.

7 Uttal, D. H, and C. A. Cohen. "Spatial thinking and STEM education: When, why, and how?" In *Psychology of learning and motivation, 57*, 147–181, 2012. Wai, J., D. Lubinski, and C. P. Benbow. "Spatial ability for STEM domains: Aligning over 50 years of cumulative psychological knowledge solidifies its importance." In *Journal of Educational Psychology, 101*(4), 817–835, 2009. Walker, C. M., E. Winner, L. Hetland, S. Simmons, and L. Goldsmith. "Visual thinking: Art students have an advantage in geometric reasoning." In *Creative Education, 2*(01), 22–26, 2011.

8 Uttal and Cohen, 2012; See also Hambrick, D. Z., J. C. Libarkin, H. L. Petcovic, K. M. Baker, J. Elkins, C. N. Callahan, and N. D. LaDue. "A test of the circumvention-of-limits hypothesis in scientific problem solving: The case of geological bedrock mapping." In *Journal of Experimental Psychology: General, 141*(3), 397–403, 2012.

MEASURING SPATIAL THINKING IN ARCHITECTURE: THE VALUE OF PSYCHOMETRIC TESTS

Thomas and Noah Shipley

What insights might psychometric tests—that is, tests designed to measure specific mental skills—provide into the role of spatial thinking in architecture? The architect employs spatial skills daily when reading or creating drawings; thinking through the puzzle-pieces of program, circulation, and building systems; or when picturing events that unfold over time, such as flows of light, water, or people. Different levels or steps of the design process likely require different types of spatial thinking. Initial massing and sketching of spaces requires one type of thinking, while detailing an entrance requires another.[1] Spatial skills even come into play during the construction phase. Architects must check the progress of building against construction documents as well as their own mental model, and sometimes what may start out as quality control quickly turns into on-the-fly spatial decision-making when changes are required.

Surely, not every architect is initially competent at all of these spatial tasks. Psychometric tests may help us understand individual variations in spatial skills. But what one does with the knowledge that some individuals have more spatial skill than others depends, in part, on whether one believes spatial thinking is supported by a fixed capacity or a learned capacity. Hereafter, we intentionally use *spatial skill* in place of *ability* because the term *spatial ability* subtly conveys a fixed individual attribute—one's capacity to reason about space. However, there is scant evidence that an individual's spatial skills are fixed for life.

Where one falls on the believing-spatial-skills-are-fixed-versus-malleable continuum appears to be cultural, with some STEM disciplines (e.g. physics) leaning toward the fixed and others (e.g. geology) toward the malleable. This cultural divide is starkly evident in the contrast between surgery and dentistry.[2] The admissions officer in a surgery program uses a spatial test to ask, "Who is likely to succeed in surgery?" and admits only those who do well on the tests. The admissions officer in a dental program uses a spatial test to ask, "Who is likely to struggle in dentistry?" and guide those who do poorly on the tests to improve their spatial skills by taking specific courses.

In both the sciences and humanities, research has found that the greater the endorsement of brilliance (a fixed ability) as important in a profession, the greater the gender disparity and the lower the proportion of African Americans in that profession. While the researchers did not collect data for architecture, the proportion of new licenses for women is 36%, and 2% for African Americans, according to 2016 data from National Council of Architectural Registration Boards. This puts architecture in the middle of the natural sciences and in the bottom quartile for humanities.[3] Although these statistics reflect structural inequality, they are also consistent with architecture's historical celebration of the "genius" architect (e.g. Le Corbusier, Frank Lloyd Wright etc.), which treats excellence in architecture as a fixed quality. The research argues for architecture schools to consider the dentistry teaching model and use psychometric tests to guide students toward courses that train critical skills. Thus, we encourage the reader to set aside any preconceived assumptions about the immutable nature of spatial reasoning in architecture, and embrace a growth mindset as a matter of opportunity—perhaps even equity—and offer three queries to illustrate the *opportunities* all architects, students and masters, might find in psychometric tests of spatial skills.

How can people with high levels of spatial skills anticipate challenges when communicating with people with lower skill levels?

Spatial tests can reveal the range of individual differences in a skill. Aware of such differences, the mindful designer can avoid biases that could introduce errors. For instance, some people struggle to understand sections. One cause of this difficulty appears to stem from assumptions about how forms project in and out of the section. Figure 1 illustrates a common error in mental cross-sectioning. While the cinnamon swirl appears to project straight into the section, a cut into the bread reveals that its orientation varies. Observers experience a strong bias (akin to a visual illusion), assuming that planes intersecting the cut of a section, such as the swirls in a slice of cinnamon bread, project perpendicularly back into the volume. Although an expert in section

1   Newcombe, Nora S., and Thomas F Shipley. "Thinking about spatial thinking: New typology, new assessments." In John S. Gero (ed.), *Studying Visual and Spatial Reasoning for Design Creativity*, 179–192. Dordrecht: Springer, 2014.

2   Hegarty, Mary, Madeline Keehner, Cheryl Cohen, Daniel R. Montello, and Yvonna Lippa. "The role of spatial cognition in medicine: Applications for selecting and training professionals." In G.L. Allen (ed.) *Applied Spatial Cognition: From research to cognitive technology,* 285–315. Mahwah, NJ: Lawrence Erlbaum Associates Publishers.

3   Leslie, SJ, Andrei Cimpian, Meredith Meyer, and Edward Freeland. "Expectations of brilliance underlie gender distributions across academic disciplines." In *Science* 347, No. 6219, 262–265, 2015.

1 A slice of cinnamon bread in section. The cinnamon swirl seen on the surface gives no indication of the orientation of the cinnamon as it extends into the slice. The cinnamon swirl indicated with a circle on top image may appear to go straight in, but as can be seen on the lower image, which is a slice into the bread, the swirl does not go straight in.

2 A test item created by diagonally slicing and moving pieces of the letters "rpepd." Geologists are adept at mentally rearranging the fragments to report the original letter sequence.

sembling broken objects—a spatial skill required in geology. Geologists excel at mentally reassembling broken objects, because in order to understand the past they must mentally reverse the changes that have occurred in rocks over geological time. Psychometric tests could potentially highlight architects' strongest spatial skills—skills they may have taken for granted. Such self-insight could allow architects to mindfully apply those skills to assorted spatial problems, and may also smooth workflows by anticipating potential areas of miscommunication.

How can practice be used to improve spatial skills?

The architectural practitioner asks, "How can I improve my reasoning about space?" or "How well am I teaching my students/staff to reason about space?" Studies of spatial reasoning in student and expert scientists have found a range of skills within each level, but have also found that these spatial skills can improve with practice.[4] Architecture students (and architects), upon reflection, will likely recognize that they have gotten better at reasoning about spaces over the course of their tenure in the discipline. These observations suggest that all practitioners of architecture, from first-year students to lead designers, may find opportunities to improve their spatial thinking. Every aspect of the architectural craft requires mentally manipulating space, and psychometric tests can offer guidance on how best to practice this skill. Since the ideal psychometric test question has been designed to isolate a spatial skill, through practice of a specific spatial skill, one may develop the associated "mental muscle."

What questions and opportunities might arise when one reexamines spatial skills in relation to the practice of architecture? One architectural studio at the Harvard Graduate School of Design attempted to do just this. The course, offered in 2019 by Professor Jungyoon Kim, focused on sectioning. Specifically, students sought to understand how inferences are made about 3D space from sections, in order to highlight individual differences in section-reading skill,

construction is unlikely to make such an error in spatial reasoning, important others, such as clients or builders, may be prone to this error. As such, practitioners should be aware of the potential for miscommunication.

What are architects good at?

Experts driven to create something both new and functional must push the limits of spatial reasoning. As such, experts in a field as spatially complex as architecture may possess heretofore unrecognized skills. Here, again, is an opportunity for psychometric tests. Scientists can use psychometric tests to search for categories of spatial skills that support specific tasks. Cognitive science research using psychometric tests has proposed categories that include: mentally navigating through a space, mentally visualizing how something would appear from a specific vantage point, mentally rotating an object, and mentally bending, slicing, and breaking objects.

To give the reader a sense of how a test might identify the building blocks of spatial reasoning, consider Figure 2, which comes from a test designed to measure skill in reas-

---

4   Uttal, David H., Nathaniel G. Meadow, Elizabeth Tipton, Linda L. Hand, Alison R. Alden, Christopher Warren, and Nora S. Newcombe. "The malleability of spatial skills: A meta-analysis of training studies." In *Psychological Bulletin* 139, No. 2, 352–402, 2013.

and to understand how disciplines other than architecture make use of sections. By focusing on the section as a spatial skill, students in the course crossed disciplines to better understand the nature of their own practice. More generally, architects can begin to transcend traditional disciplinary silos by highlighting the role of spatial skills in training and practice.

3 Jungyoon Kim, *Diagrammatic and descriptive section can elucidate critical concepts in ways that other types of drawing can not easily illustrate. In this vertical panoramic section, spatial distribution of the Baikal Lake agents are depicted in a single view.* (Student: Yeon Angela Choi, MLA 2019 Harvard GSD)

TRAINING SPATIAL ABILITIES

Andri Gerber

Based on the experience of designing these tests, and on the outcomes of our testing sessions, the question arose as to how we could translate this knowledge back into architecture. How can one transform something designed for measurement into something to help training and improve the measured ability? While our test was de-contextualized, it seemed to make sense that, as a training instrument, it should be applied to real examples of architecture. Thus, the next step comprised selecting examples of buildings and urban configurations that would fit the different tests precisely. These were chosen from both famous and less well-known historical examples of architecture and urban design, and as such, this book also serves as a pleasant collection of references for architecture students. Along with our four tests, we also decided to include a test of visualization with cross-sections (the Mental Cutting Test)—as this test worked particularly well for architects—and to adapt it to our architecture references as well (Mental Cutting Test, Architecture). These references were transformed in order to better fulfill the requirements of the test. Functionality was thus weighted more than realism. At the same time, they could not be too far removed from the architectural nature of the references. These were therefore also rendered as volumes, "ignoring" the inside of the buildings—except in the case of the Indoor Perspective Test. This was done in order to reduce the mental load and the "noise"—as it is referred to in these tests—to allow the subjects to focus on relevant matters. Yet one default in our adaptation was unavoidable: being closer to architectural references augmented the possibility to solve certain tests analytically, as the number of clues automatically increased. This problem seems unavoidable, but might be reduced in future re-workings of these tests.

The reader might forgive me if I take the liberty of sharing three personal anecdotes, as they might illuminate where my interest in space and psychometric tests comes from and the adaption of the latter for this book. The first anecdote goes back to my childhood, when after changing schools and having a terrible new teacher, I lost my passion for biology and was sent to a career counselor. After several days of testing my rather average skills, it emerged that I have strong spatial abilities. This lead to the suggestion to study architecture—or forestry engineering—which I then followed. At this time it was already well understood that architecture had something to do with spatial ability—associated with other skills—and in my case, a talent for drawings.

The second anecdote occurred during an apprenticeship in an architectural office in Geneva, where my boss introduced me to the 3D game Tetris on a computer, and told me to play it as much as possible in order to increase my spatial ability. Here, too, I was struck by this insight about the importance of spatial abilities as well as the possibility to enhance them by gaming![1] Finally, when beginning to study architecture, I enrolled in programs in Milan and Florence. In both institutions, there was an admissions exam that was supposedly able to identify those more suited to becoming an architect. In Milan, the test was purely logical, based on playing cards and identifying missing ones; in Florence, on the contrary, the test was only based on general culture. Neither test convinced me about what an architect is really supposed to know—although without doubt general culture is fundamental—and led me to the question of what would comprise a good test (if such a test is at all necessary …). I encountered similar tests time and time again—for example, at the entry exam for the École Speciale d'Architecture in Paris—and they always left me puzzled about their efficacy.

It should be underscored that our test was never intended to be used as an admissions exam, but if used, it should be accompanied by other measures and other tests in order to have a more holistic insight into any candidate. At the same time, I do believe that our test would make a more effective measure than the tests I have personally experienced so far. Similar tests are already used in Switzerland in the qualifying examination for the architectural draughtsman apprenticeship, even if no unified measure exists thus far. Neither applied nor technical architectural schools in Switzerland have such an admissions test. It is in this context that the idea of a concrete application for training arose—and to avoid exactly this misuse of our work as admissions material.

In general, it is clear that the kind of test and training material based on graphic abstraction completely misses the haptic dimension of architecture and its spaces, yet this is a necessary compromise that was unavoidable from our perspective. The test and the training material covers only one of the many aspects of architecture—this should be clear to everybody working with it. This book is intended to merge the literature on training material for tests, such

---

1   Gerber, Andri, and Ulrich Götz (eds.). *Architectonics of Game Spaces. The Spatial Logic of the Virtual and Its Meaning for the Real.* Bielefeld: transcript, 2019.

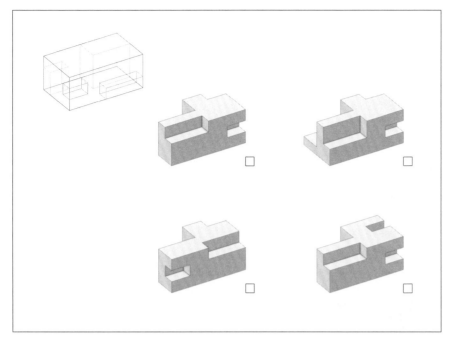

1 Anita Cantieni, Laura Franceschini, Nina Hofmann, Tu Lan,
Negative and Positive Volumes, 2019

as spatial reasoning tests, and as such, we attempted to present the book less as an architectural book—and, as such, with an elaborated cover graphic design—and more as a book that should be used again and again, and should help the user not to be intimidated. The test had a time limit, but the tasks here were not designed to be solved under time pressure. The examples in this book have no time indication, yet progress of the student can be measured in their increased solving speed and should be considered. Thus, when doing the exercises, one should record the time and compare it to successive sessions. All tests should be done without making sketches, markings, or by measuring things—only mentally.

Developing new Tests with Students

Parallel to the development of our own tests, I held seminars with architecture students on the development of other possible tests for architectural spatial abilities. Students were asked to come up with their own tests, based on what they think is important in relation to spatial ability and architecture. The students were first introduced to our tests and discussed the relevant literature on the matter, before starting to identify specific spatial abilities they thought were relevant. One group, for example, considered the difficulty that architecture students often have when they have to prepare a mold for casting gypsum. So their test is about finding the correspondence between a negative volume, which is represented in wireframe, and one of four positive volumes, represented with shaded surfaces.

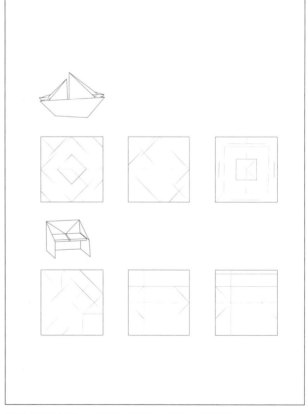

2 Vivienne Galliker and Meret Heeb, *Origami*, 2019

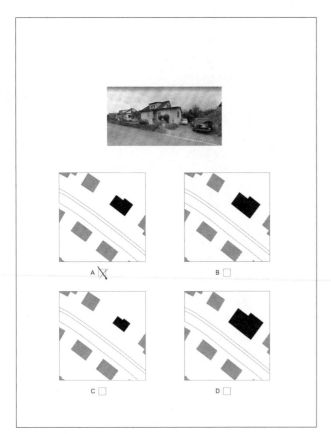

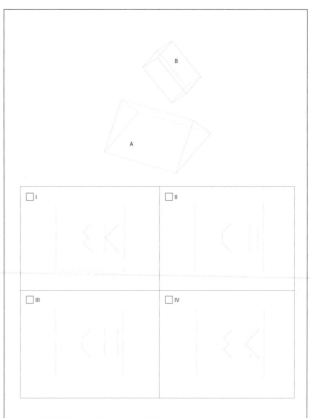

3 Adrienne Enz, Monika Grabski, Céline Ryffel, *Zooming*, 2019

4 Aurore Delory, Tobias Lenggenhager Rebekka Anliker, *Negative Volumes,* 2019

Another group started working on an existing test, the Paper Folding Test, in which paper with holes is folded and the subject has to identify the correct unfolded form. The students extended this idea of a mental ability capable of translating this process of folding and unfolding through origami, and thus creating a three-dimensional form of the folding.

Another group worked on a very specific architectural challenge: the relationship of a plan to an image, in particular concerning the correct scale. Out of four differently scaled objects, the subject has to choose the one matching the image. So this test is not about recognizing the correct shape between plan and image, but about ascertaining the correct scale of an object. The scale then has to be put in relation to the size of the plot and the other buildings.

The final group worked on an extremely elaborate and difficult test, based on the intersection of complex volumes. Two volumes are presented; then, one volume is inserted into the other, and this intersection becomes a negative volume. The task is then not to imagine the negative volume as a volume, but how the new volume looks in plan. Even though probably too complicated and implying more than one mental process, this task is very close to the complex mental processes of architects.

Having students reflect upon what kind of mental abilities they consider relevant and to develop a corresponding psychometric test was a very powerful tool, enabling them to reflect on the matter through the making of something. The students took each test conceived by their colleagues, and a cohort of non-architects was brought together as a control group. Even if statistically not relevant, in all of the tests, architects outperformed non-architects. It was very enriching for the students to witness a real application of their work and to have this backed-up by statistical findings that confirmed—with all due precautions—the assumption our group had made.

I hope this book will have the same effect.

In this test you will see an urban arrangement in axonometric. Your task is to imagine yourself standing in two points "A" and "B" on the ground and to decide how the two scenes would look from these two points. You have to choose from four possible perspectives. All perspectives are correct but only one will correspond to the point "A" and one to the point "B."

Try to solve the example below, based on a project by Spanish architect Ricardo Bofill:

Ricardo Bofill, *Les arcades du lac,* Saint-Quentin-en-Yvelines, 1982

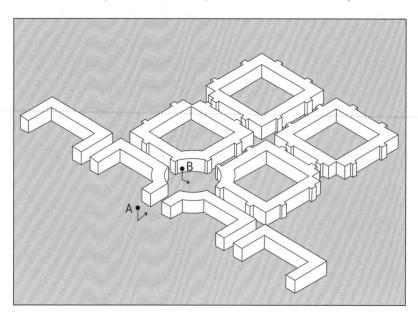

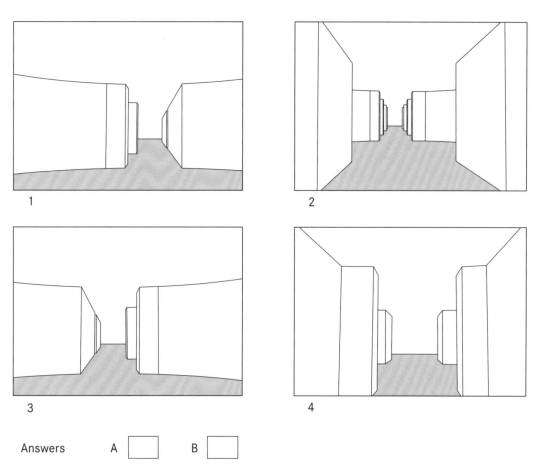

1

2

3

4

Answers   A ☐   B ☐

Point „A" corresponds to Perspective 2. Point „B" corresponds to perspective 1. Wrong perspective 3 corresponds to point 3 indicated in the plan below. Wrong perspective 4 corresponds to point 4 indicated in the plan below. Only one perspective corresponds to „A" and one to „B".

Ricardo Bofill, *Les arcades du lac,* Saint-Quentin-en-Yvelines, 1982

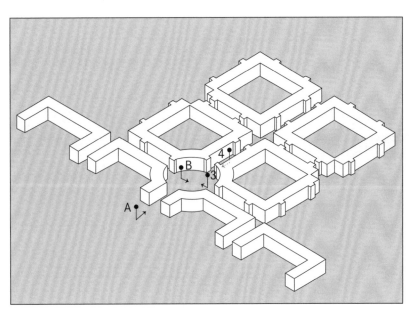

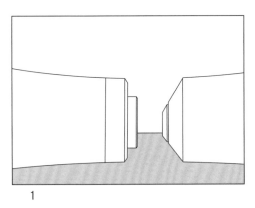

1

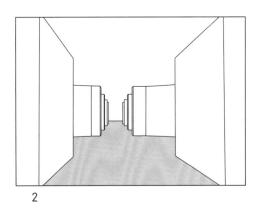

2

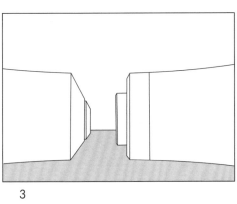

3

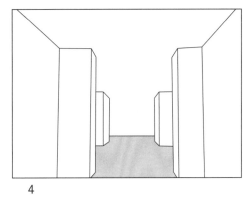

4

Answers   A   2   B   1

Francesco di Giorgio Martini, *Ideal City,* circa 1478

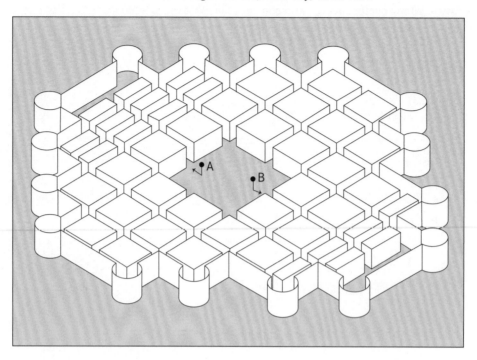

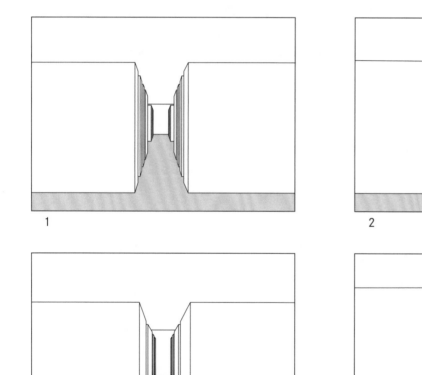

1

2

3

4

Answers   A ☐   B ☐

Aldo Rossi, *Cimitero San Cataldo,* Modena, 1971–84

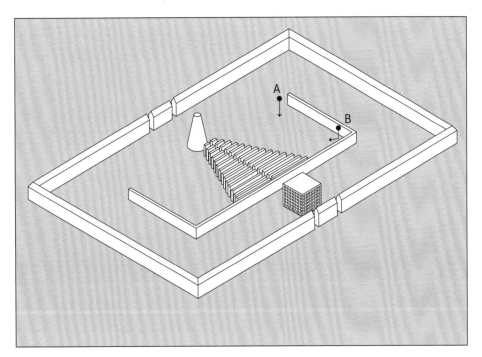

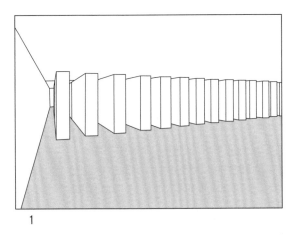

1

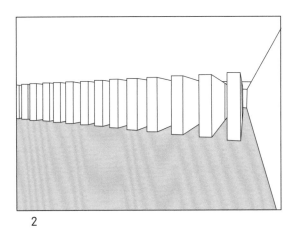

2

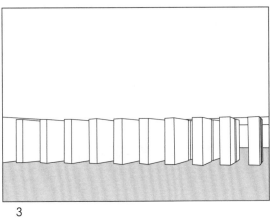

3

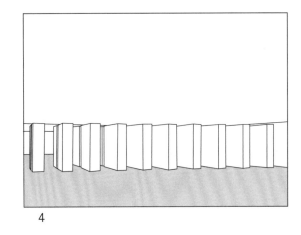

4

Answers   A ☐   B ☐

Vincenzo Scamozzi, *Ideal City,* 1615

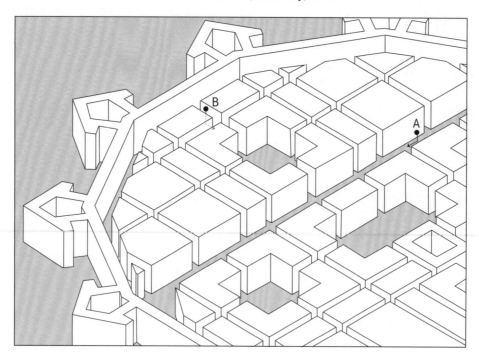

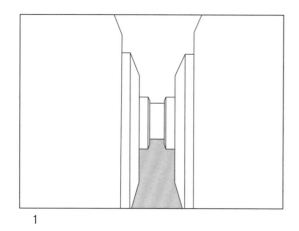

1

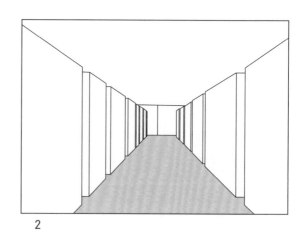

2

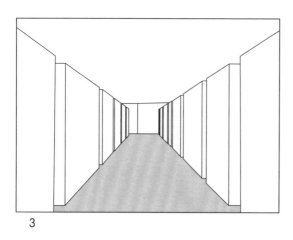

3

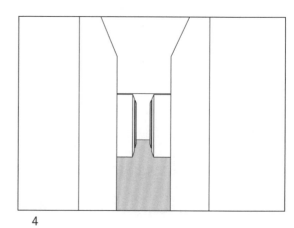

4

Answers   A ☐   B ☐

Martin Wagner, Bruno Taut, *Siedlung Lindenhof,* Berlin, 1918

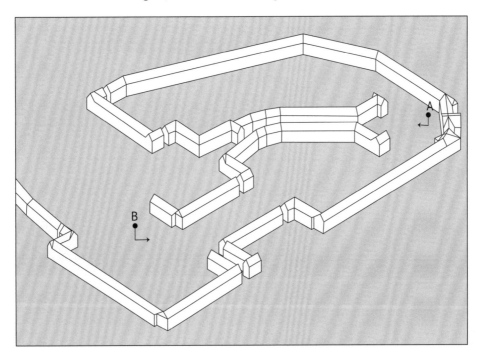

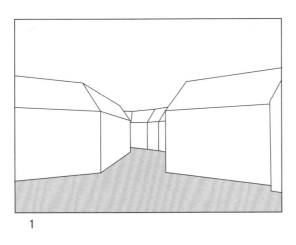

1

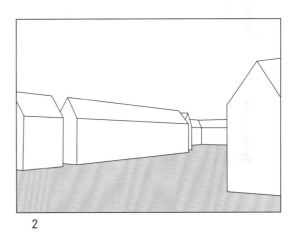

2

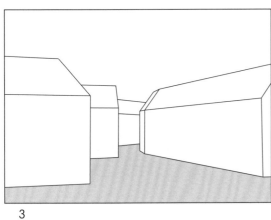

3

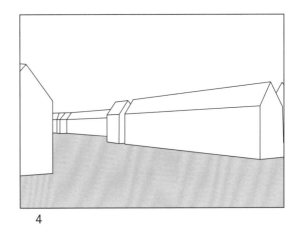

4

Answers   A [   ]   B [   ]

Villa d'Este, Rome, circa 1572

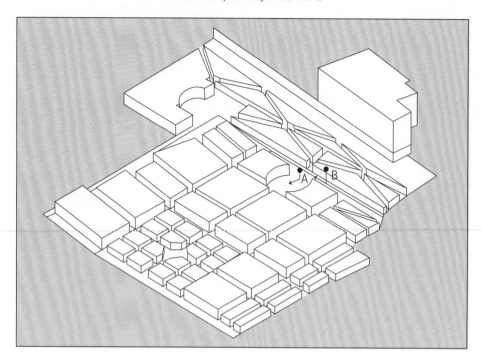

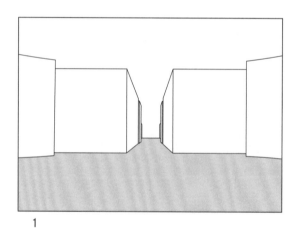

1

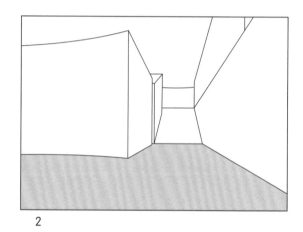

2

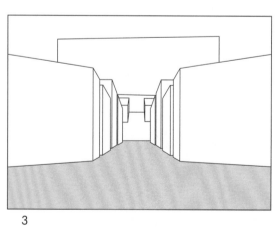

3

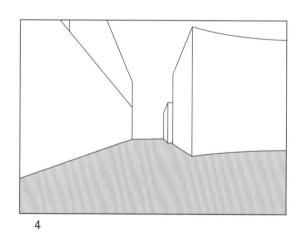

4

Answers   A ☐   B ☐

5 | 4 | 3 | 2

Lina Bo Bardi, *SESC – Fabrica da Pompeia,* São Paulo, 1986

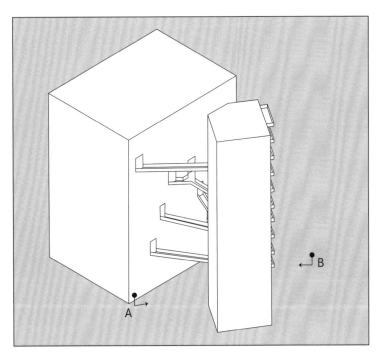

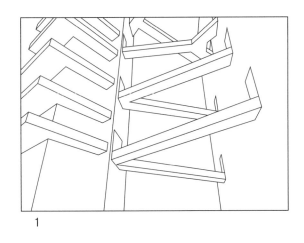

1

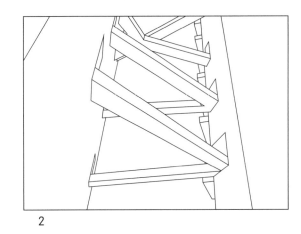

2

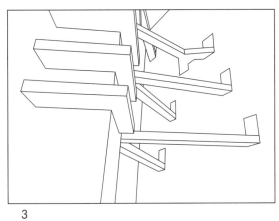

3

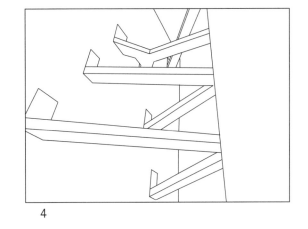

4

Answers   A ☐   B ☐

Çatalhöyük, Turkey, circa 7500–5700 BC

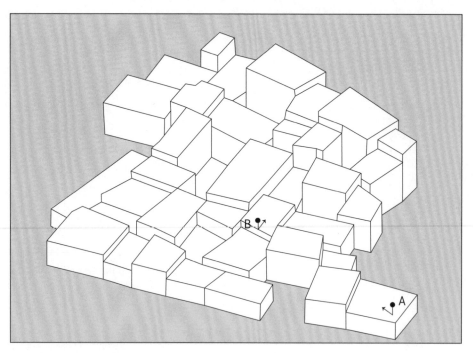

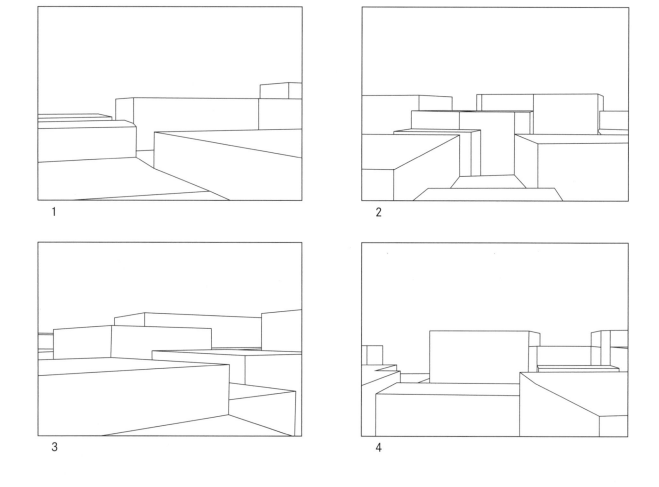

1

2

3

4

Answers   A [ ]   B [ ]

5 4 3 2

Jacques I. Androuet du Cerceau, *Project for a Place at the Pont Neuf,* circa 1578

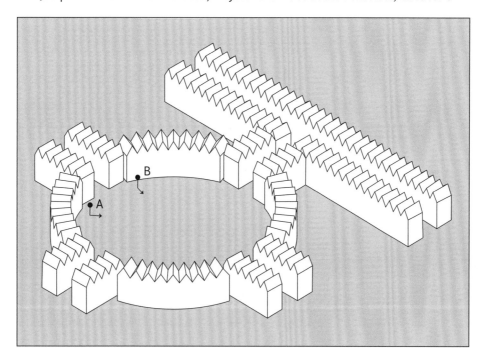

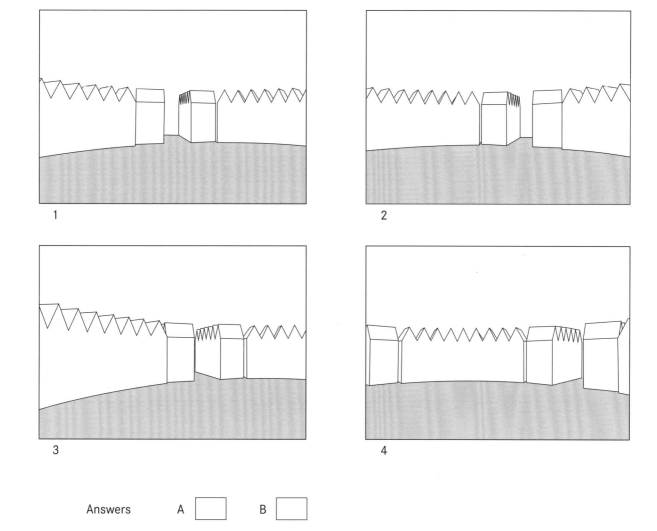

1

2

3

4

Answers   A ☐   B ☐

Steven Holl, *Spatial retaining Bars,* Phoenix, 1989

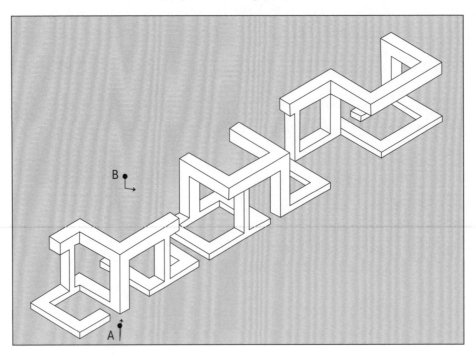

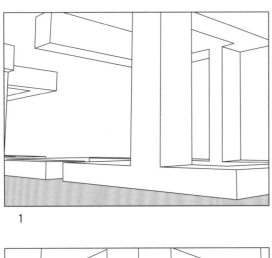

1

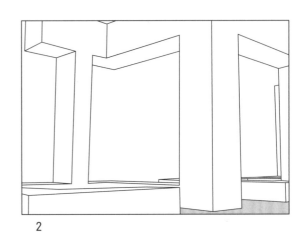

2

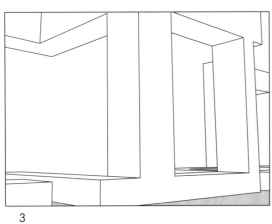

3

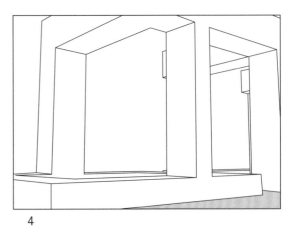

4

Answers   A ☐   B ☐

Le Corbusier, *Ville contemporaine pour 3 millions d'habitants,* 1922

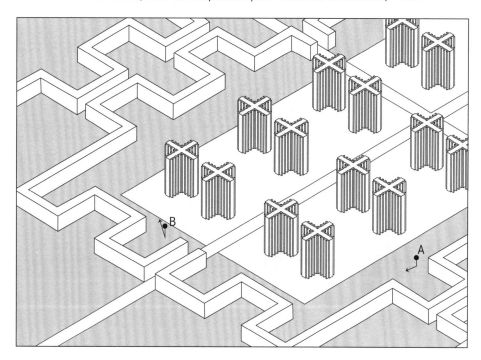

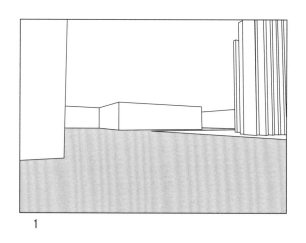

1

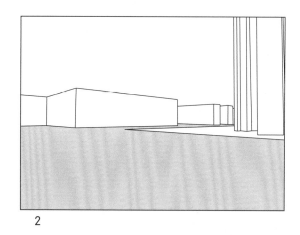

2

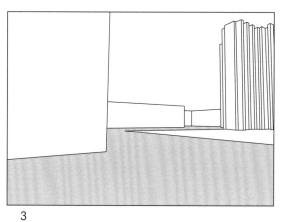

3

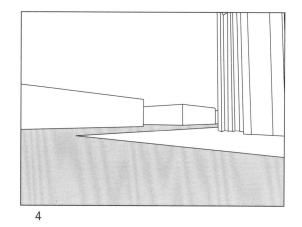

4

Answers   A ☐   B ☐

Alcide Mathieu, *Plan idéal d'une capitale modèle,* 1880

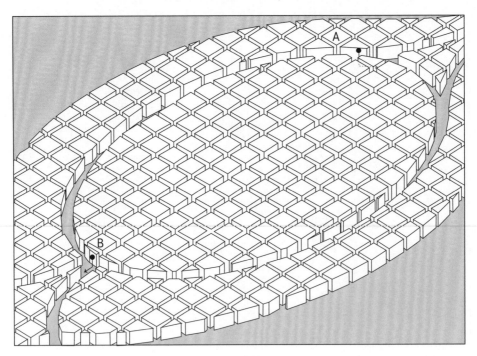

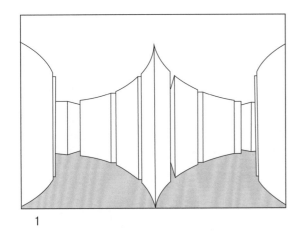

1

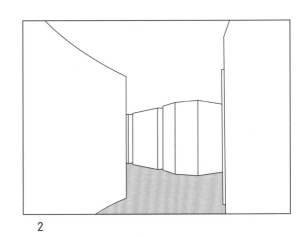

2

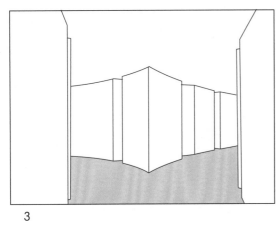

3

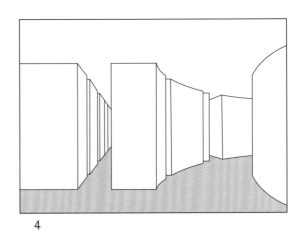

4

Answers A ☐ B ☐

Christopher Wren, *Plan for Rebuilding the City of London after the Great Fire,* 1666

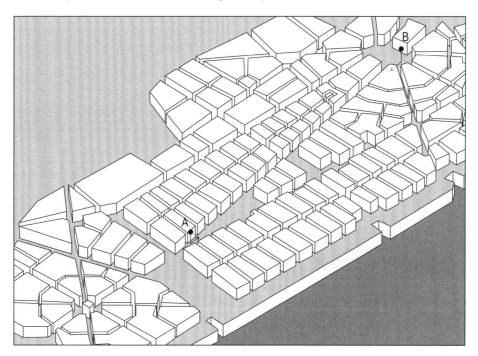

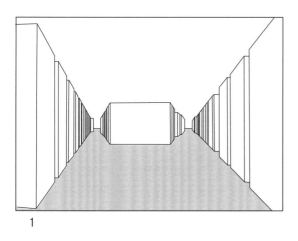

1

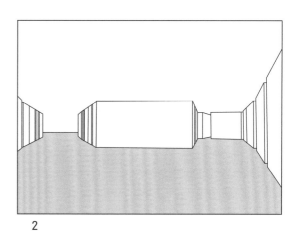

2

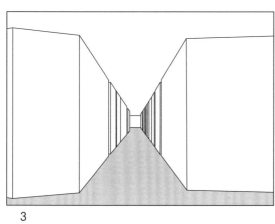

3

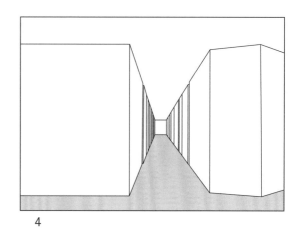

4

Answers A ☐ B ☐

Hubert Ritter, *Rundling,* Leipzig, 1930

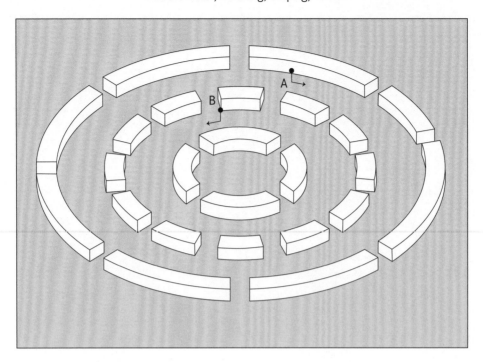

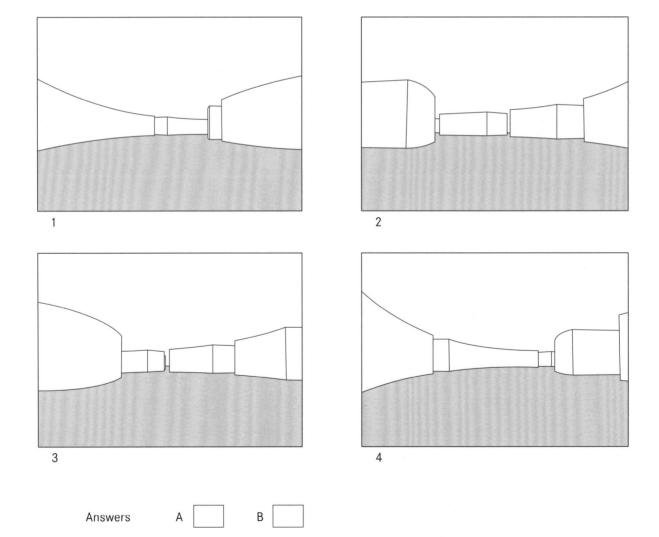

Answers A [   ] B [   ]

Ildefonso Cerdà, *Extension of Barcelona,* 1859

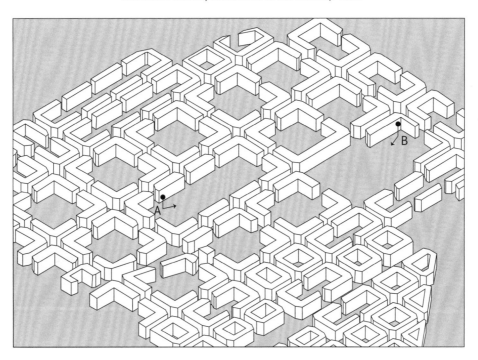

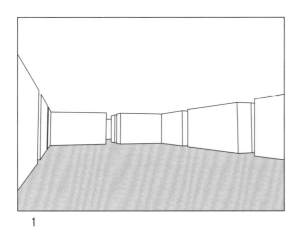

1

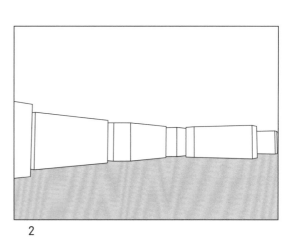

2

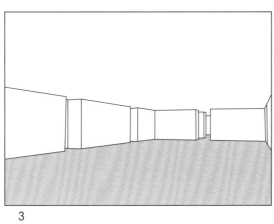

3

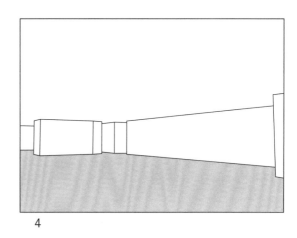

4

Answers   A ☐   B ☐

Émile Aillaud, *La Grande Borne,* Essonne, 1972

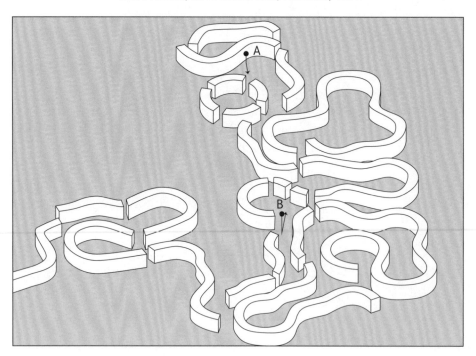

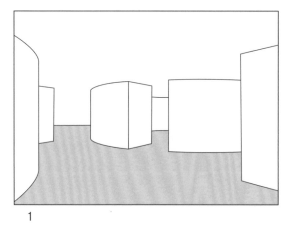

1

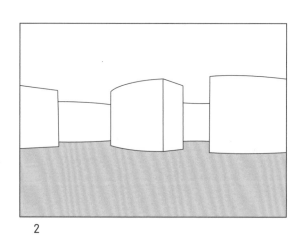

2

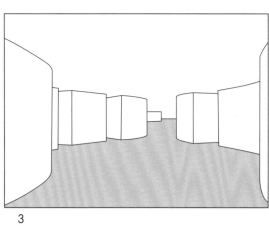

3

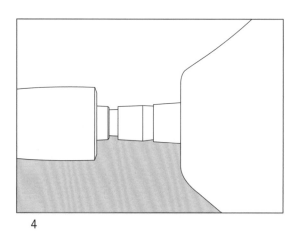

4

Answers   A ⬜   B ⬜

In this test you are given a volume shown in axonometric from two different points of view.

The task of this test is to imagine yourself inside the volume and to choose the correct view. Two letters indicate the position of the observer—first letter—and towards which angle he is looking—second letter.

You have to choose from four possible perspectives where only one corresponds to the position and direction indicated. Incorrect answers are given by perspectives taken from another point inside the volume.

Louis Kahn, *Fischer House,* Pennsylvania, 1967

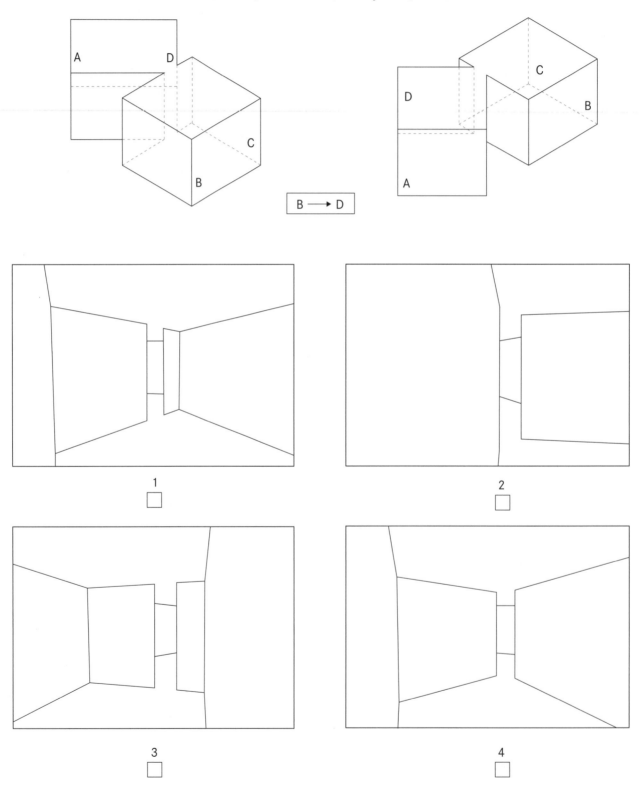

The correct answer is 1. Only there are you standing at the letter B and looking towards letter D.

In answer 2, you are standing at letter D and are looking towards the letter B.

In answer 3, you are standing at the letter C and are looking towards the letter A.

In answer 4, you are standing at the letter A and are looking towards the letter C.

Louis Kahn, *Fischer House,* Pennsylvania, 1967

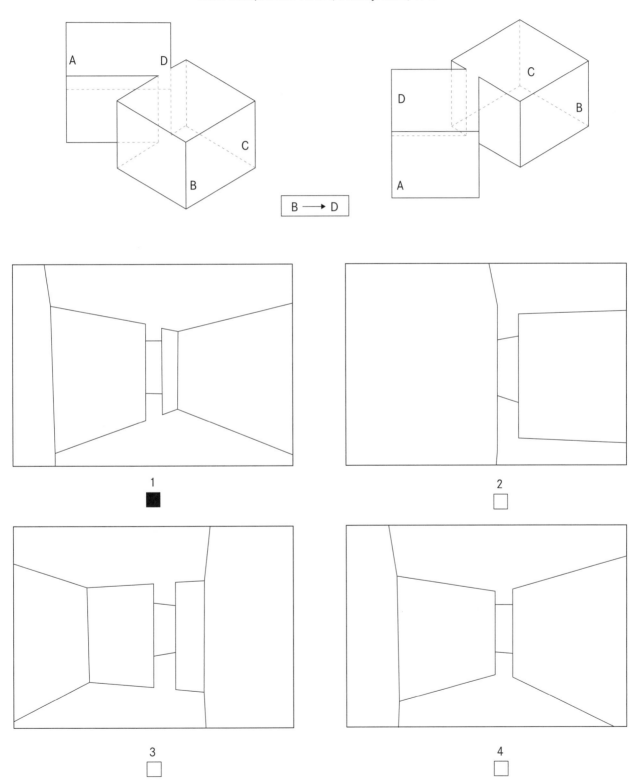

Robert Venturi, *Lieb House,* New Jersey, 1967

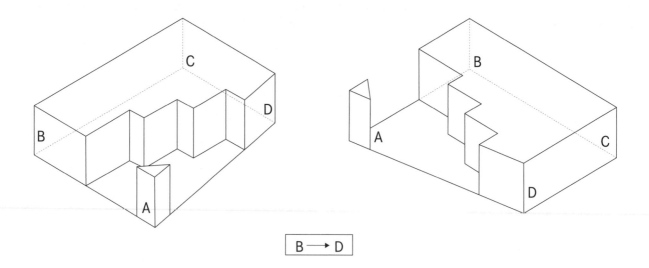

B ⟶ D

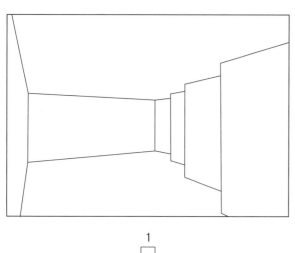

1 ☐

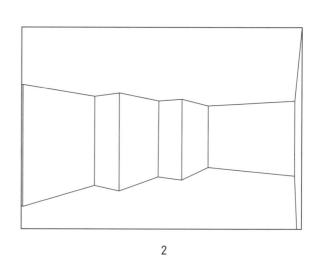

2 ☐

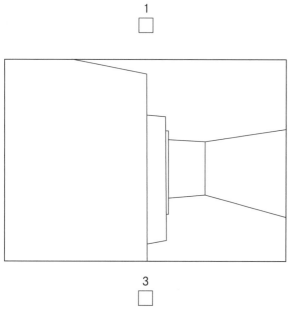

3 ☐

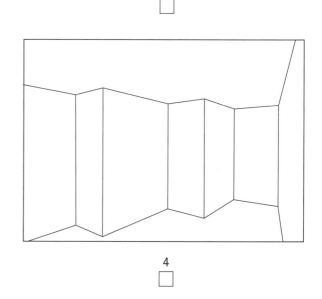

4 ☐

Valerio Olgiati, *School in Paspels,* Domleschg, 1998

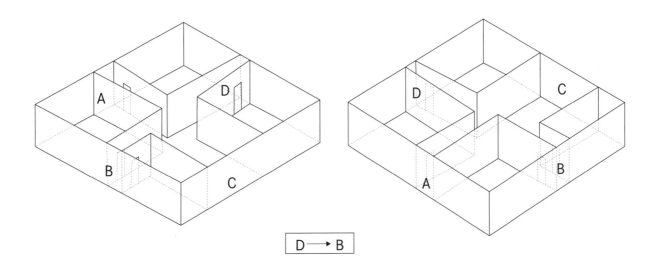

D → B

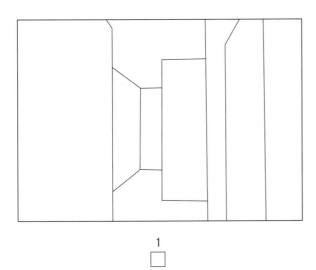

1

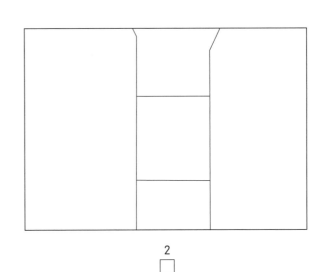

2

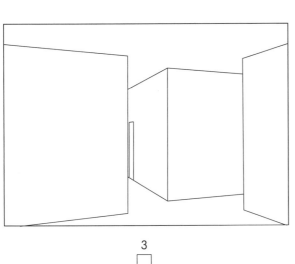

3

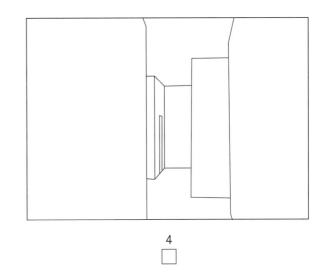

4

Gunnar Asplund, *Summer house,* Stennäs, 1937

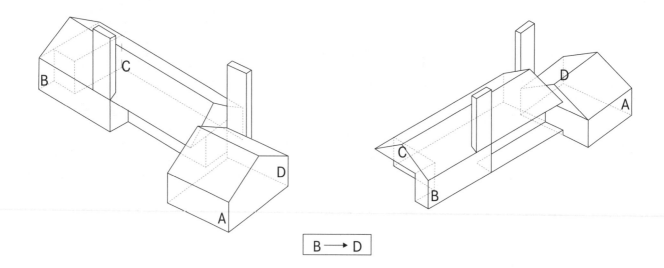

B ⟶ D

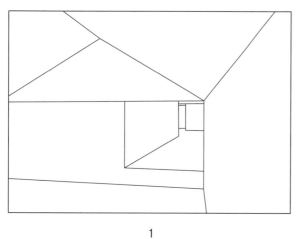

1

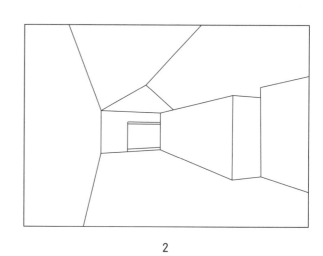

2

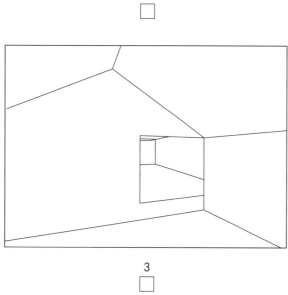

3

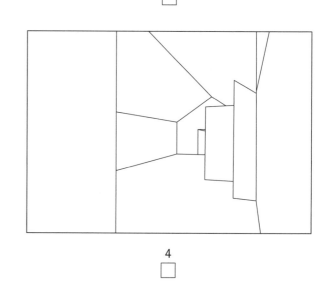

4

Peter Zumthor, *Thermen Vals,* Vals, 1998

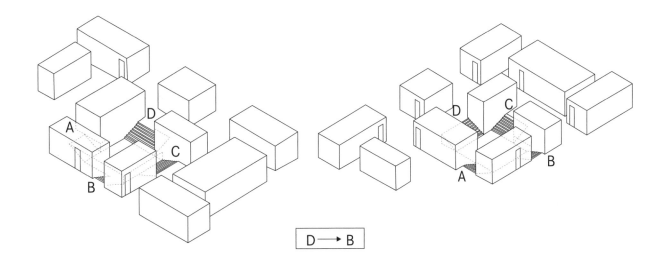

D ⟶ B

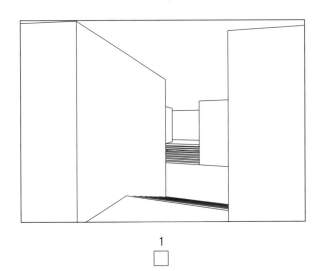

1

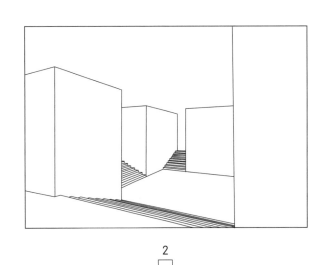

2

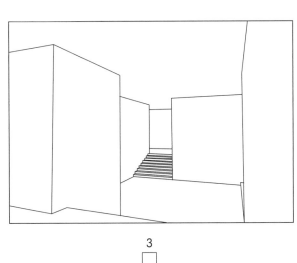

3

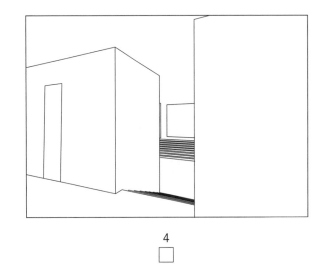

4

Álvaro Siza, *Saint-Jacques-de-la-Lande,* Rennes, 2018

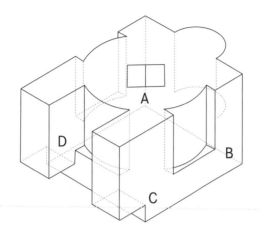

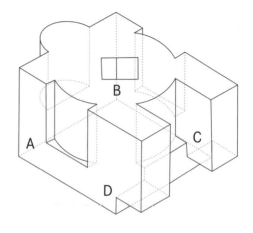

C ⟶ A

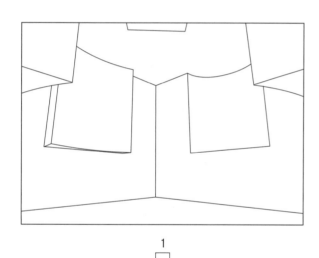

1

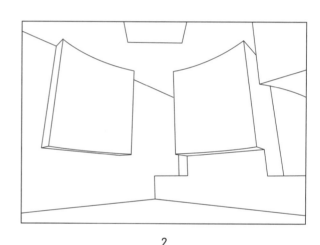

2

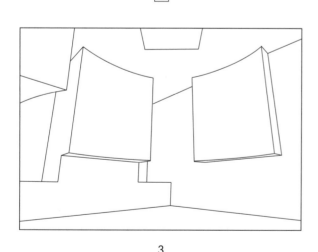

3

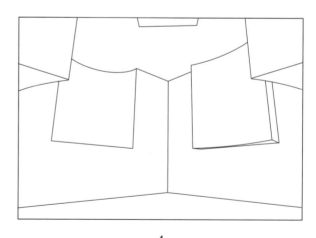

4

Myron Goldfinger, *Goldfinger House,* Waccabuc, NY, 1970

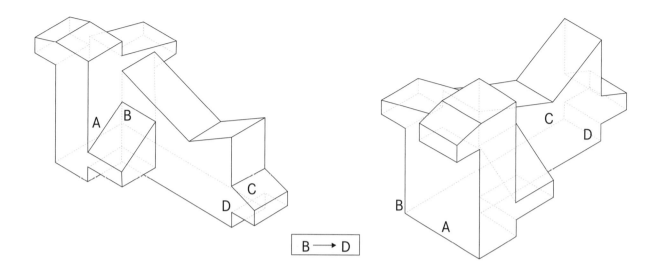

B ⟶ D

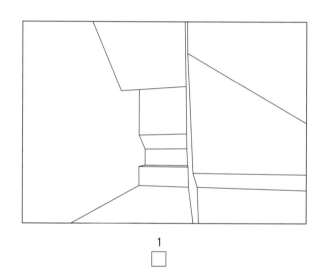

1

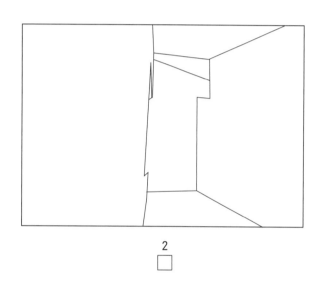

2

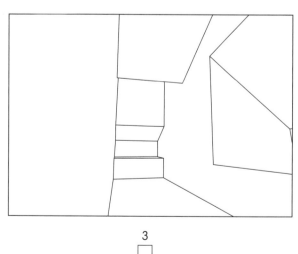

3

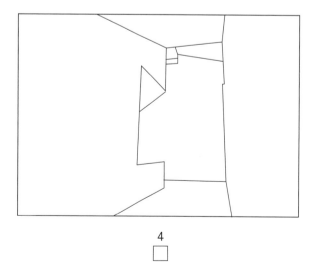

4

Valerio Olgiati, *Villa Além,* Portugal, 2014

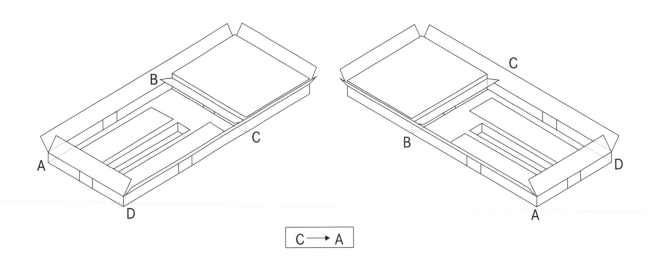

C ⟶ A

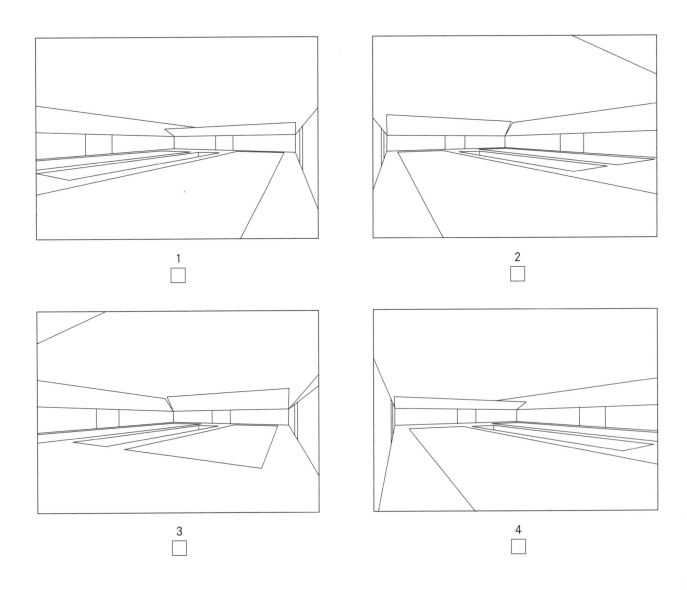

1

2

3

4

Louis Kahn, *Jewish Community Center,* New Jersey, 1959

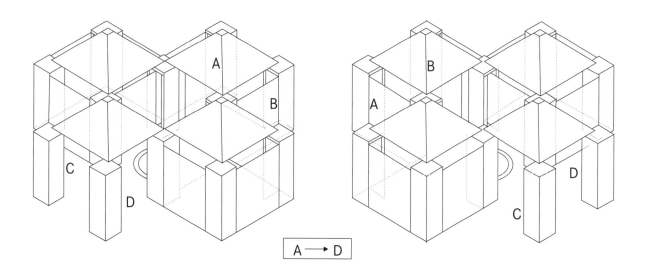

A ⟶ D

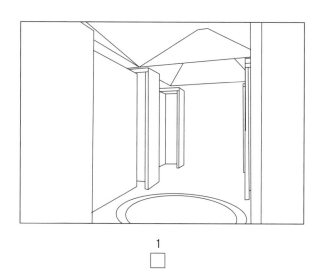

1

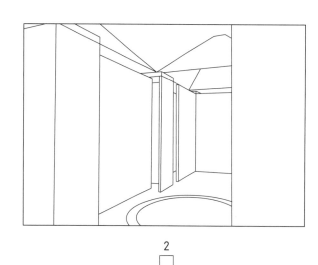

2

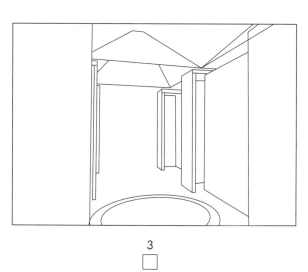

3

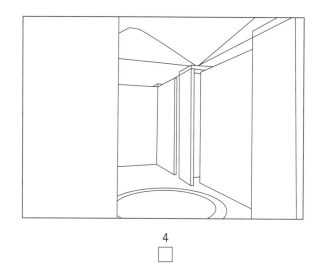

4

Rem Koolhaas, *CCTV – Headquarters,* Beijing, 2012

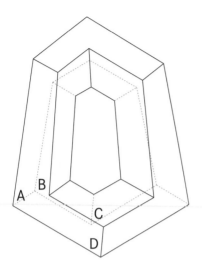

A ⟶ C

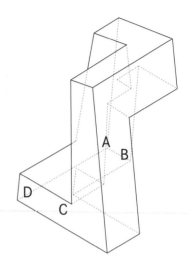

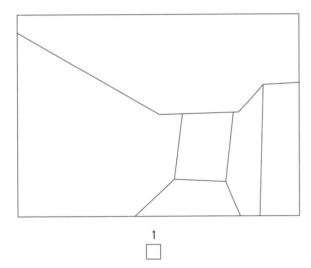

1
☐

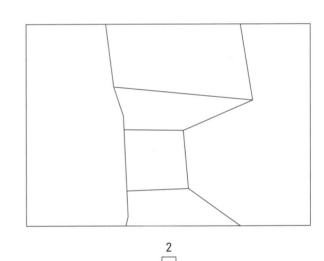

2
☐

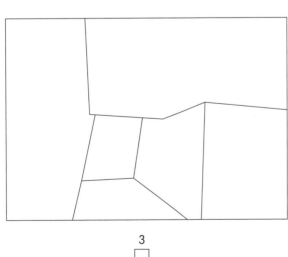

3
☐

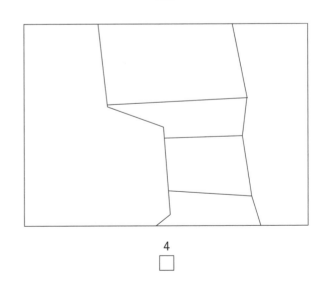

4
☐

Kazuo Shinohara, *Tanikawa House,* 1974

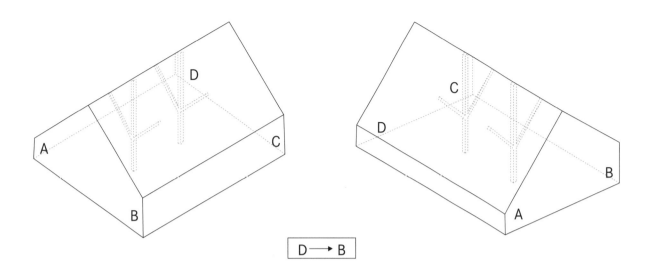

D ⟶ B

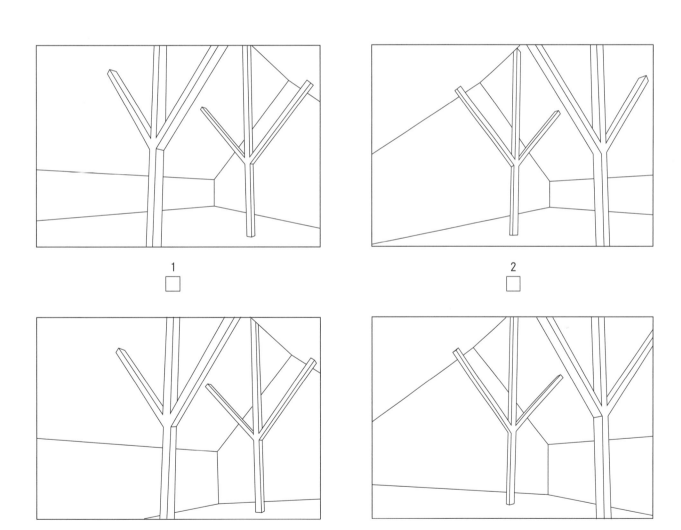

1

2

3

4

Frank Gehry, *Guest House Winton,* Minnesota, 1987

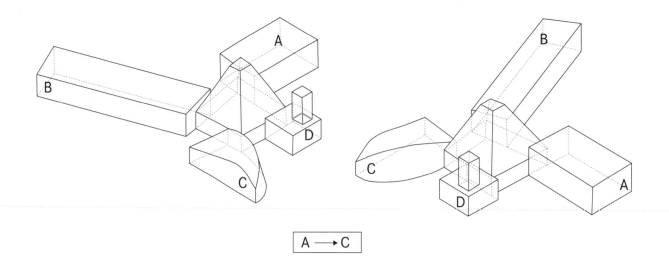

$$A \longrightarrow C$$

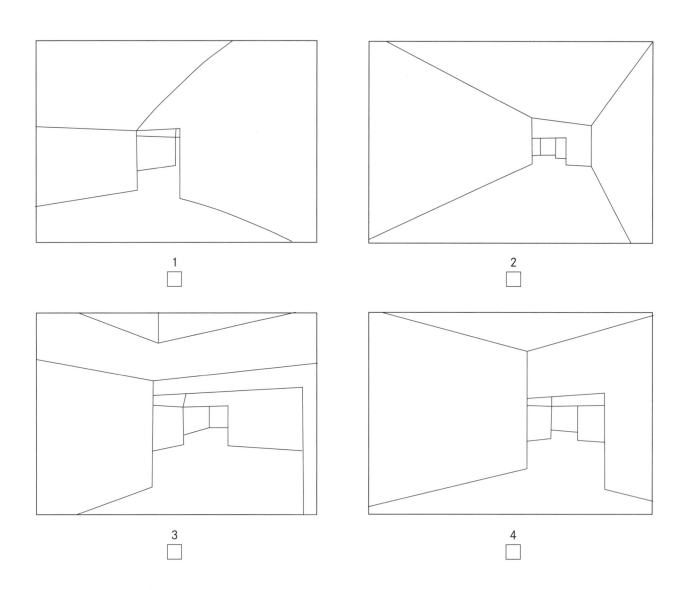

1 ☐

2 ☐

3 ☐

4 ☐

Agustín Hernández, *Architectural Office,* Mexico City, 1975

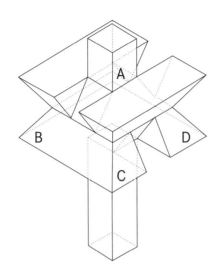

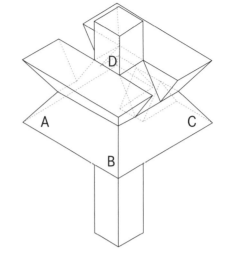

$$A \longrightarrow C$$

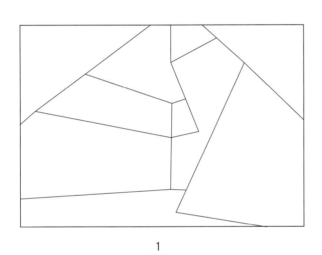

1 ☐

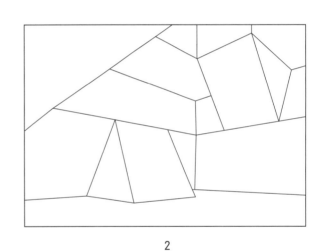

2 ☐

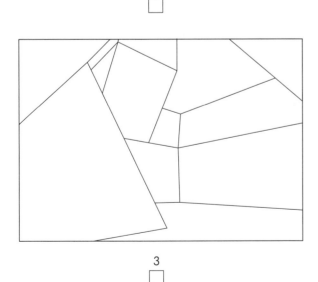

3 ☐

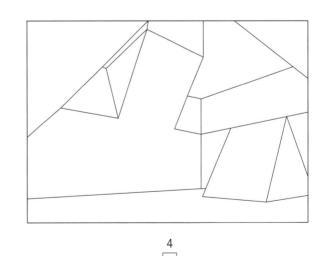

4 ☐

Iseppi-Kurath, *Viamala Gas Station,* Thusis, 2008

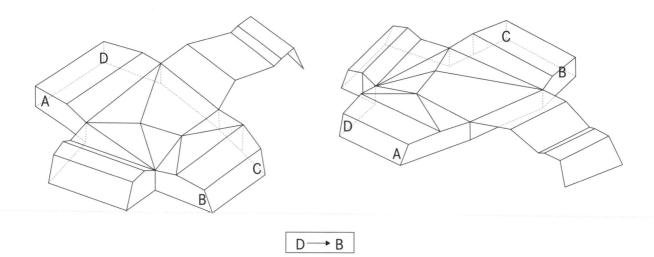

D → B

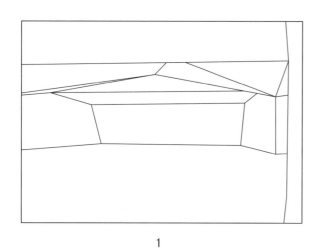

1
☐

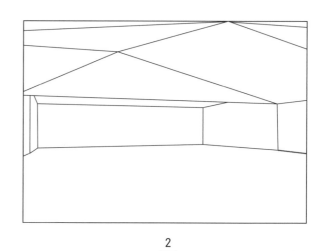

2
☐

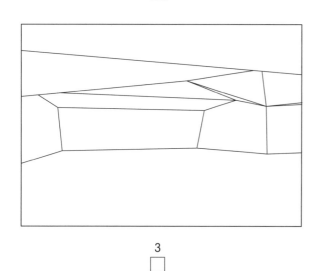

3
☐

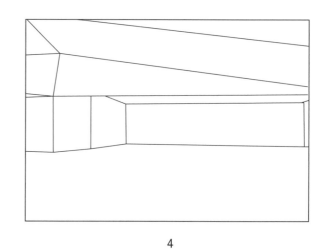

4
☐

Toyo Ito, *Tama Art University library*, Tokyo, 2007

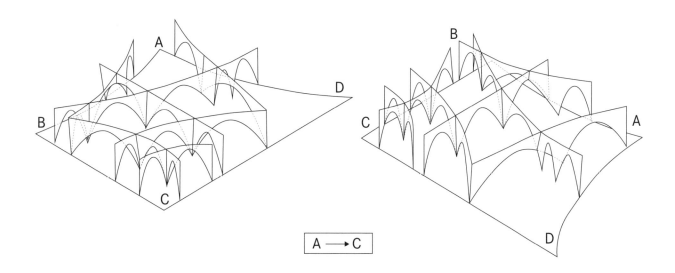

A ⟶ C

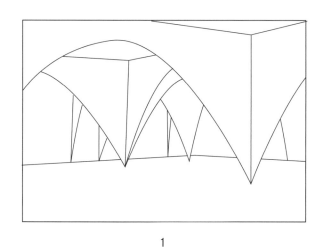

1 ☐

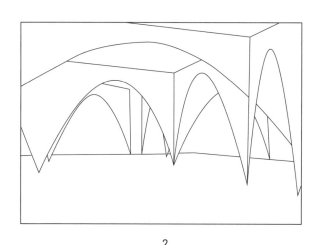

2 ☐

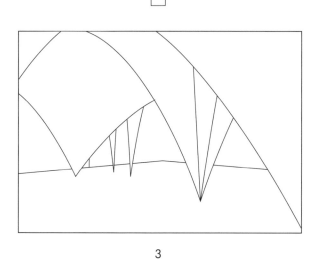

3 ☐

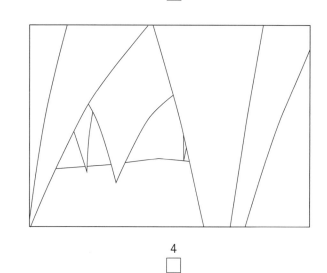

4 ☐

Pezo von Ellrichshausen, *Svara Pavilion,* Venice, 2016

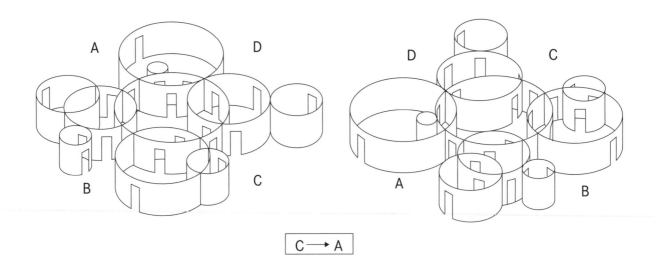

C ⟶ A

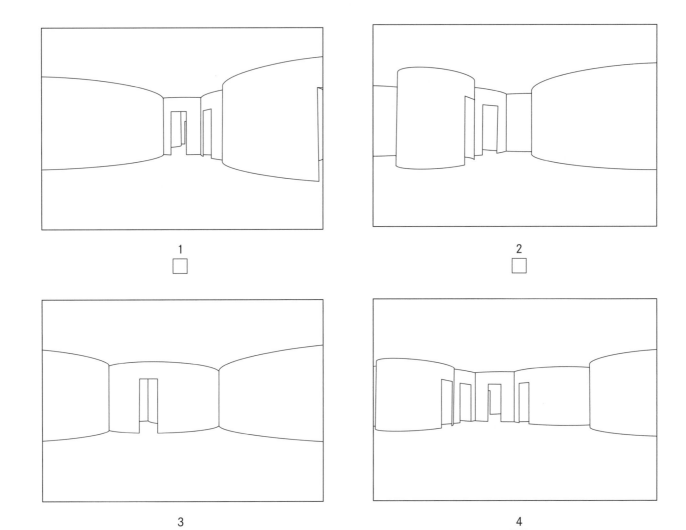

1

2

3

4

In this test you are asked to judge whether a set of smaller shapes can be packed into another large shape (target). The smaller shapes must fit exactly in the larger shape, so that no unused spaces are left in it. Note that the filling in the larger shape is possible only by mentally "moving" the smaller shapes in different directions, but not by "rotating" them.

In the following questions you will be asked to decide which set of shapes out of four given sets fits the target shape. The target is not in the same scale as the four options. Look at the example below. Which of these shapes can be composed of the set of smaller shapes at the top? Mark the answer you think is correct.

pool Architekten, *Wohnsiedlung Leimbachstrasse,* Zurich, 2005

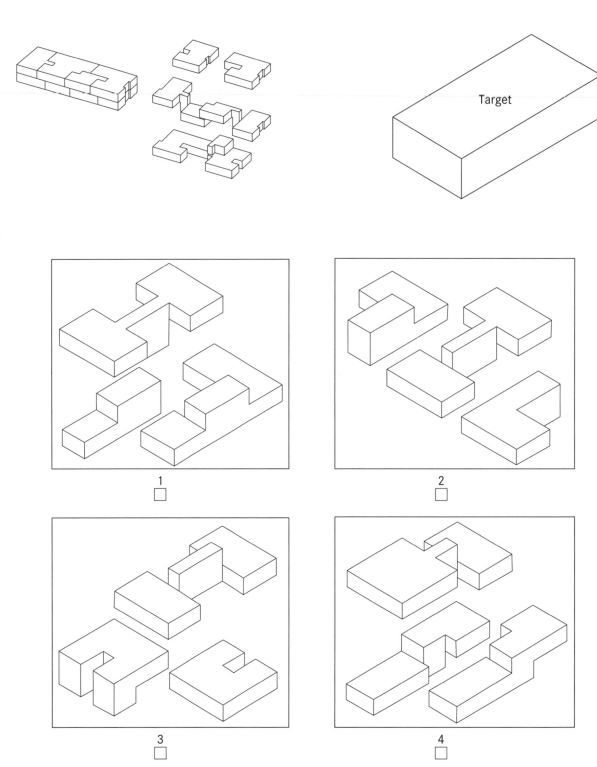

Target

1 ☐

2 ☐

3 ☐

4 ☐

The correct answer is 2. Only the three shapes in answer 2 can completely fill in the shape.

The three shapes of option 1, if connected, exceed the shape of the target (exceeding). The three shapes of option 3 do not completely fill the shape of the target (missing). The three shapes of option 4 overlap (collision). The examples following in the next pages have either three or four shapes to assemble.

pool Architekten, *Wohnsiedlung Leimbachstrasse,* Zurich, 2005

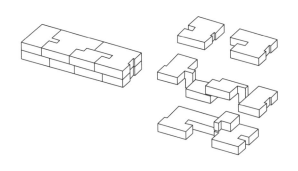

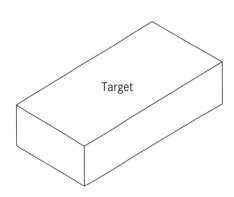

Target

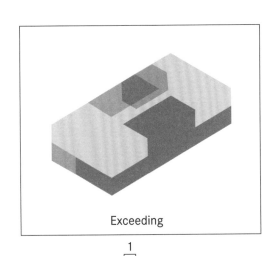

Exceeding

1
☐

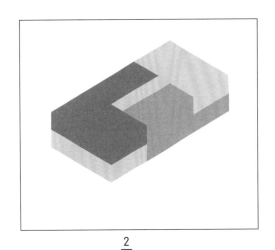

2
■

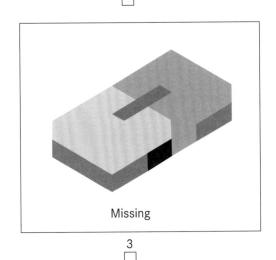

Missing

3
☐

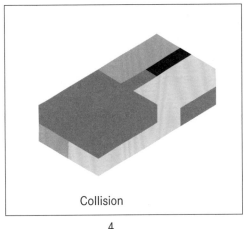

Collision

4
☐

MVRDV, *Silodam,* Amsterdam, 2003

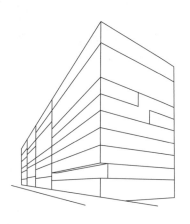

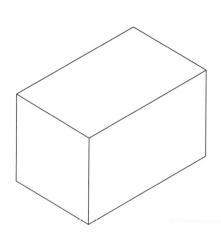

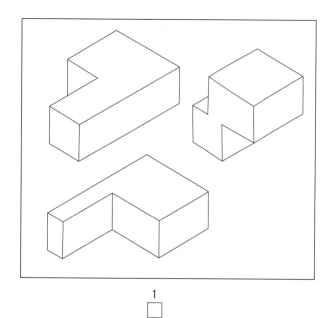

1
☐

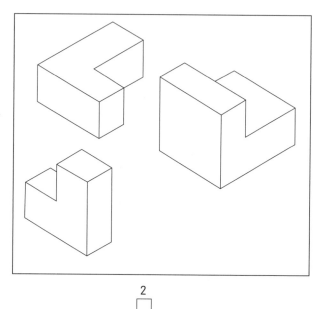

2
☐

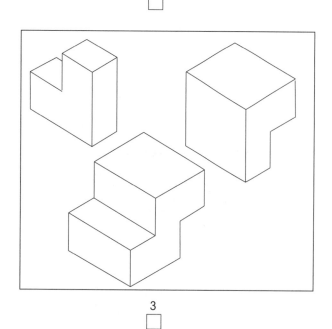

3
☐

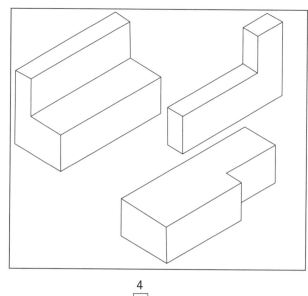

4
☐

Mario Botta, *Casa Medici,* Stabio, 1982

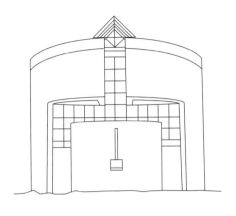

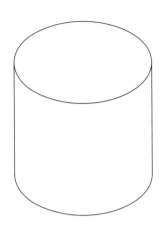

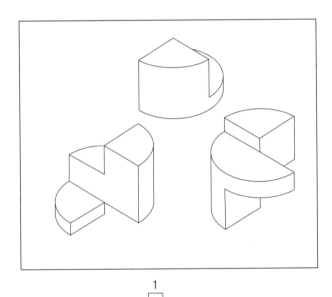

1

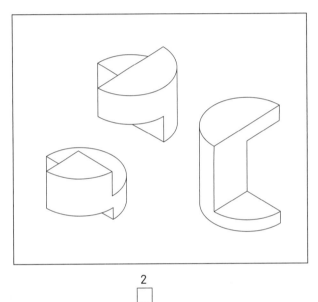

2

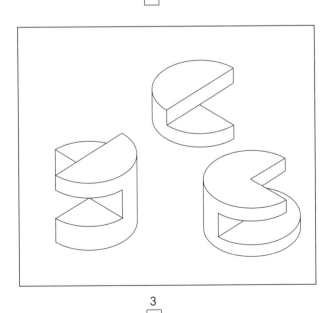

3

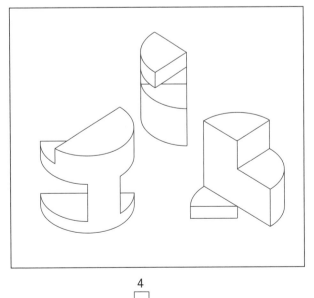

4

Kazuyo Sejima, *Kitagata Apartment Building,* Gifu, 2000

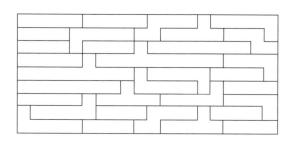

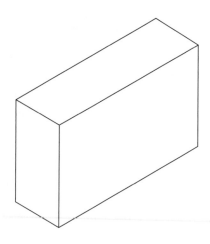

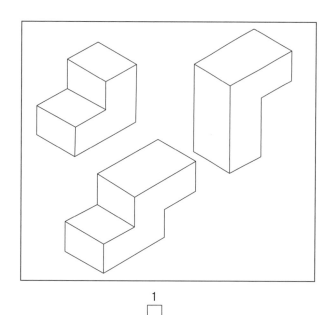

1
☐

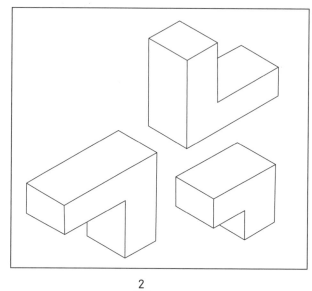

2
☐

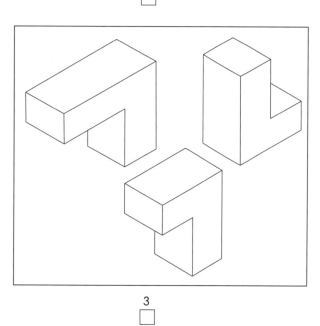

3
☐

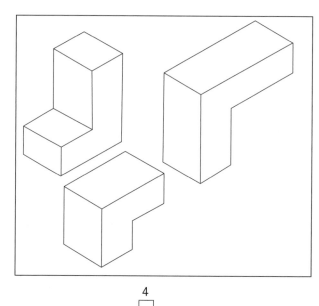

4
☐

Adolf Loos, *House Tristan Tzara,* Paris, 1926

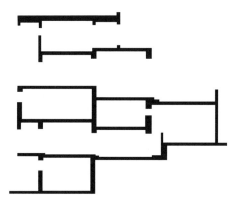

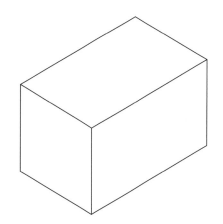

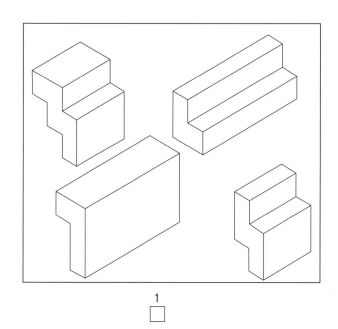

1
☐

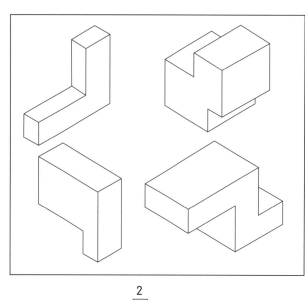

2
☐

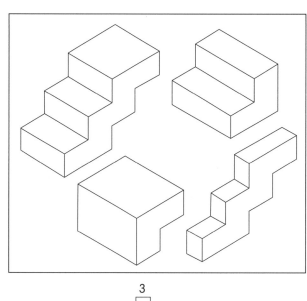

3
☐

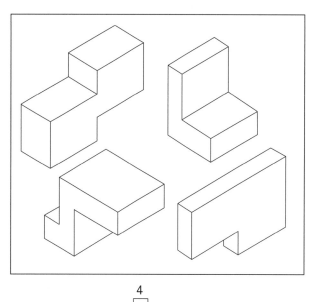

4
☐

Walter Gropius, Fred Forbàt, *Baukasten im Großen,* Dessau, 1923

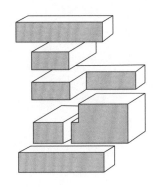

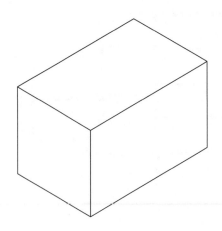

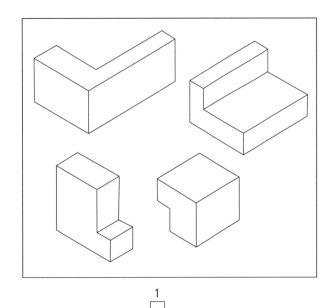

1
☐

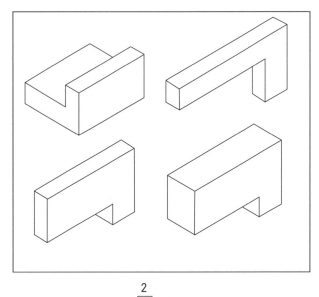

2
☐

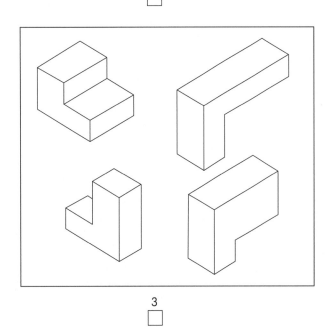

3
☐

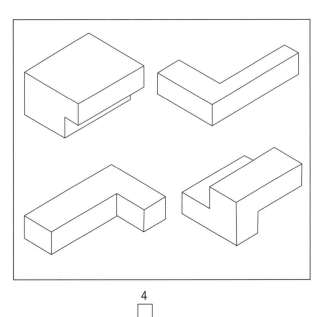

4
☐

Sou Fujimoto, *Final Wooden House,* Kumamoto, 2006

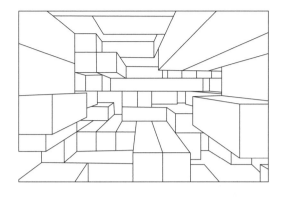
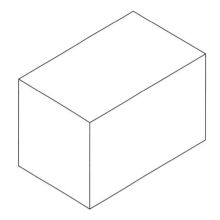

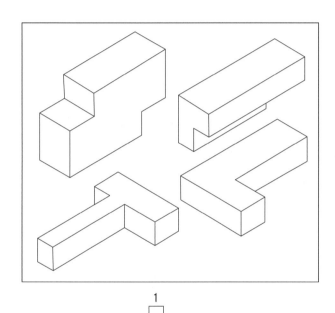

1
☐

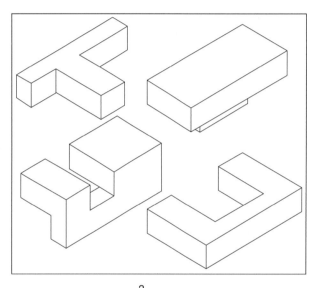

2
☐

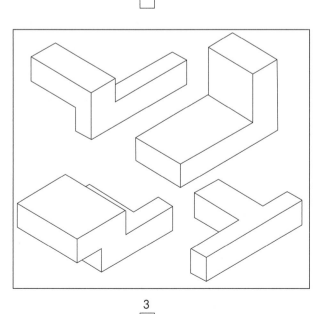

3
☐

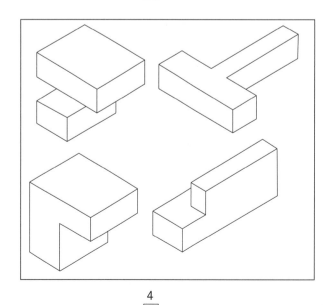

4
☐

Claude Parent/Paul Virilio, *Maison Mariotti,* Saint-Germain-en-Laye, 1970

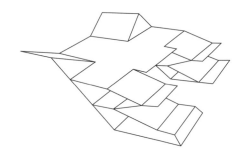
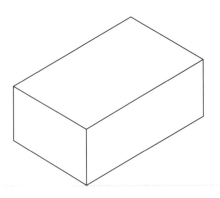

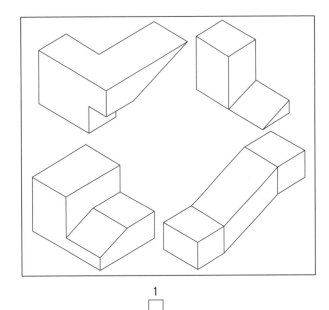

1

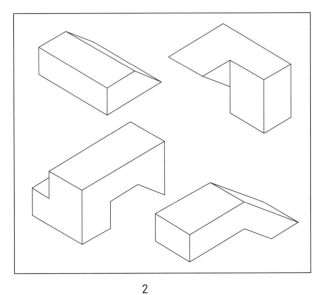

2

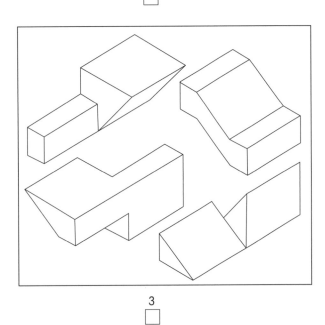

3

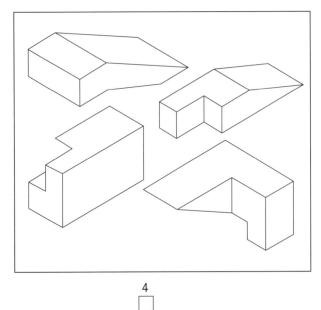

4

Raimund Abraham, *House for Musicians,* Hombroich, 1999

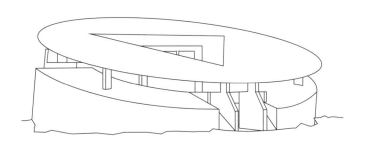

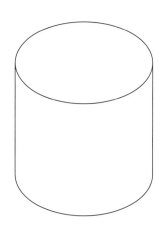

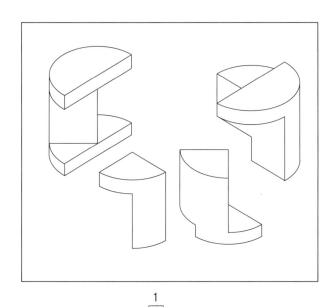

1 ☐

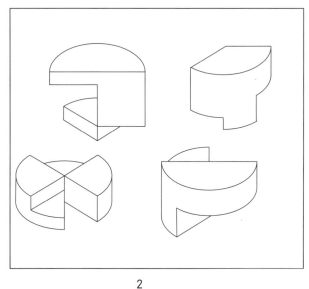

2 ☐

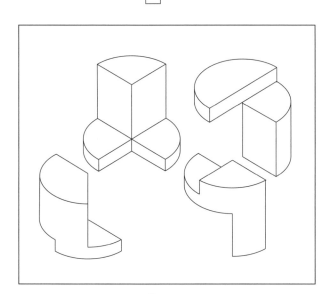

3 ☐

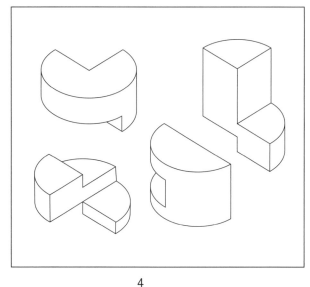

4 ☐

HHF/BIG, *Puzzle House,* Denmark, 2019

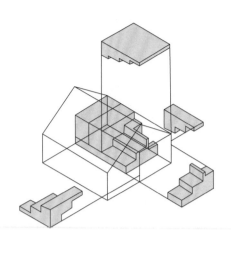

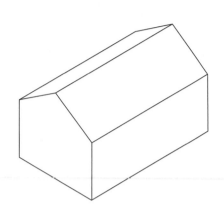

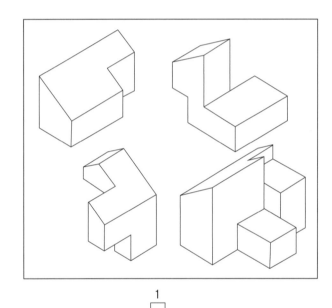

1

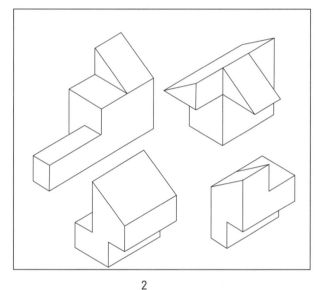

2

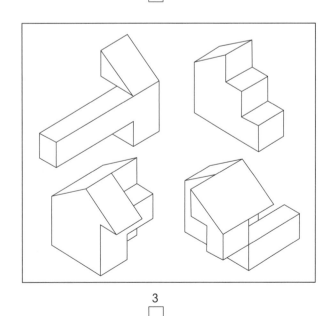

3

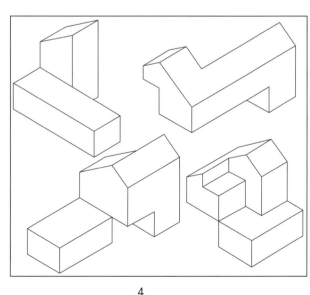

4

Paul and Blanche Mahlberg/Bruno Taut, *Dandanah,* 1920

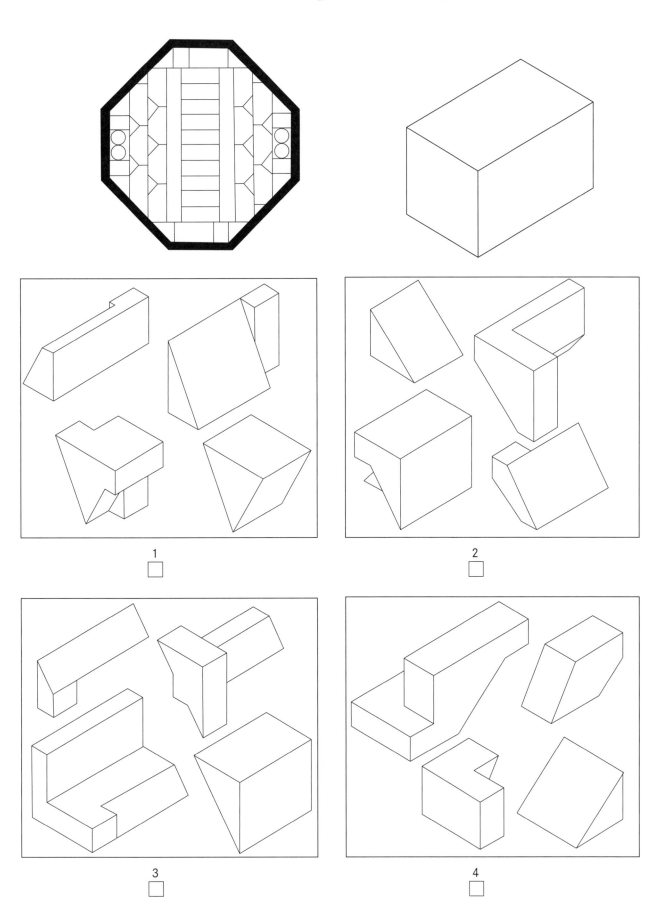

1

2

3

4

Daniel Libeskind, *V & A Museum Extension,* London, 2002

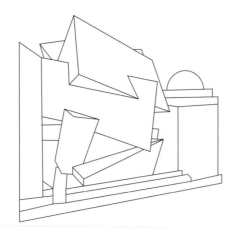

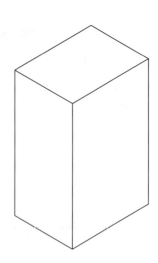

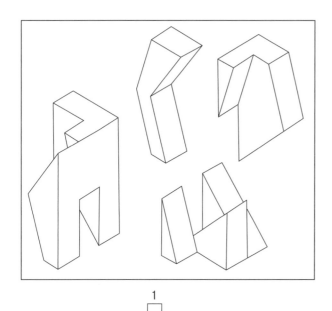

1 ☐

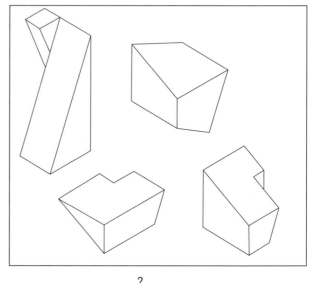

2 ☐

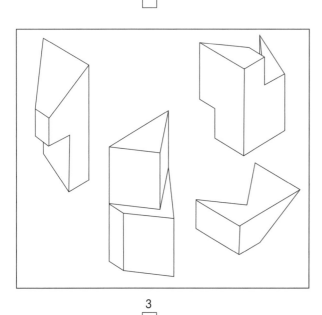

3 ☐

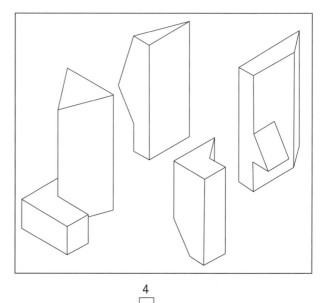

4 ☐

Rem Koolhaas, *Dutch Embassy,* Berlin, 2004

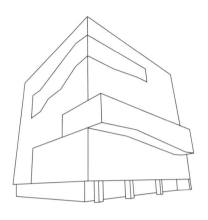
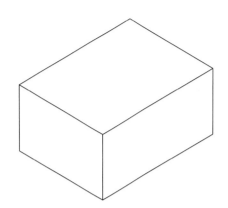

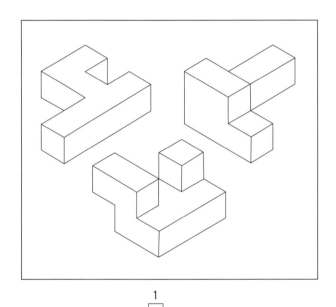

1

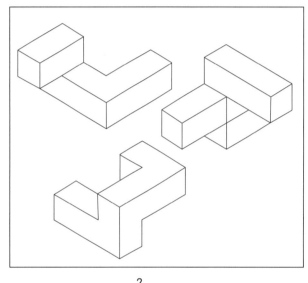

2

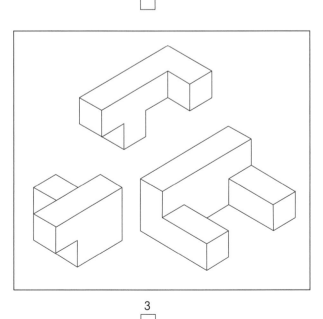

3

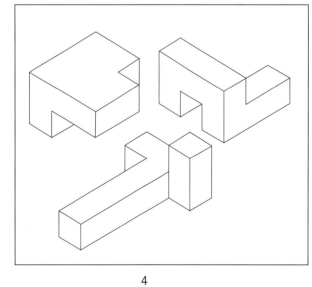

4

Ben van Berkel, *Möbius House,* Het Gooi, 1998

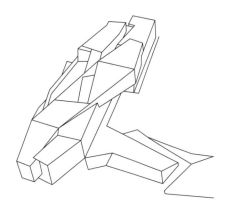

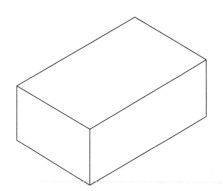

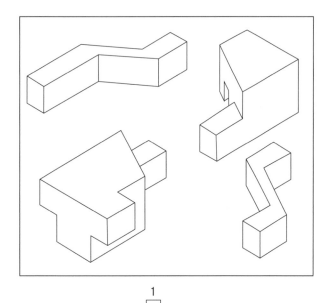

1
☐

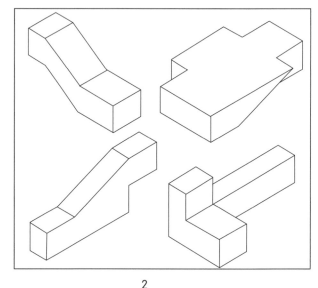

2
☐

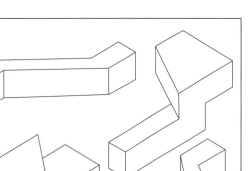

3
☐

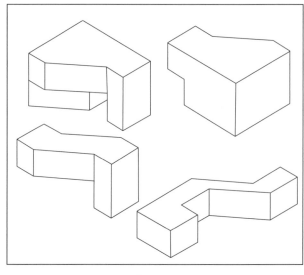

4
☐

Le Corbusier, *Unité d'habitation,* Marseille, 1952

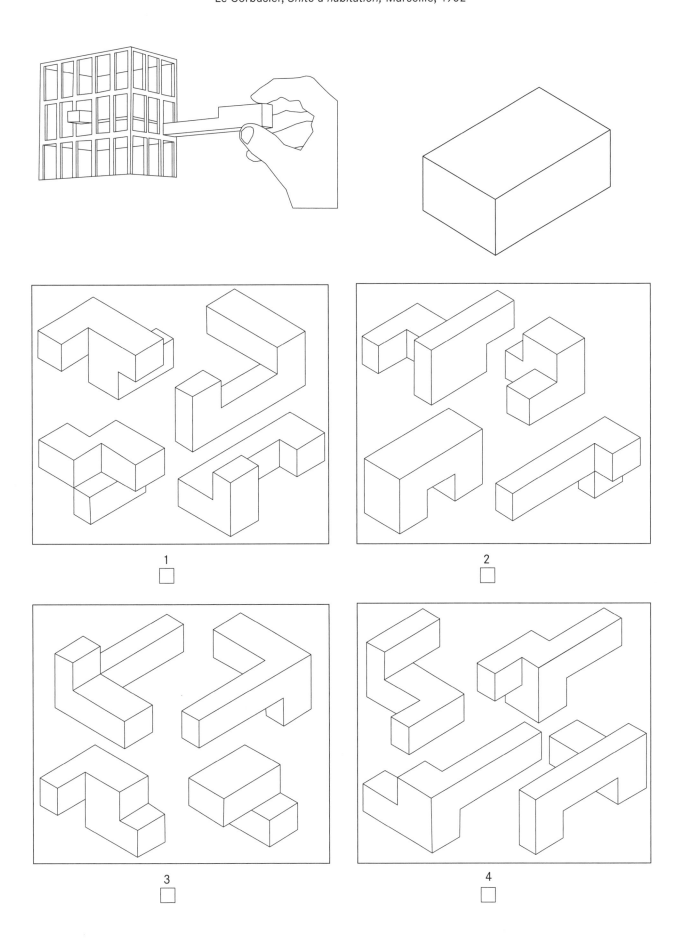

1 ☐

2 ☐

3 ☐

4 ☐

Fuhrimann & Hächler, *Haus Eva Presenhuber,* Vnà, 2007

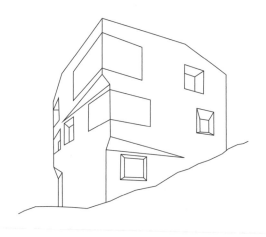 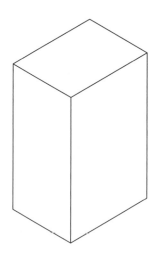

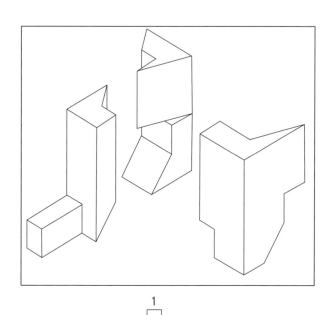

1

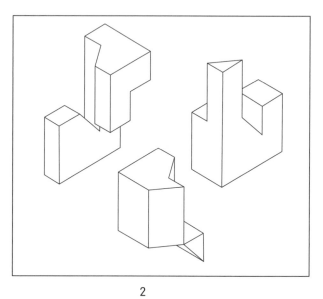

2

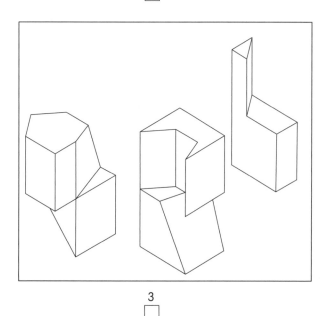

3

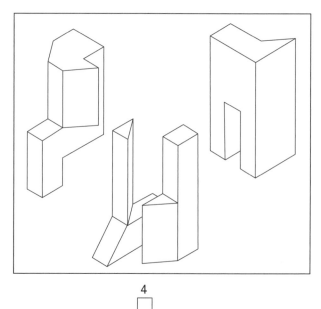

4

In this test you are asked to transform a cube according to several steps, adding or subtracting mass over the axis x, y, and z. Consequent transformations are always applied to the new volume as transformed through the precedent step. The sequence of the steps are indicated by the numbers in parenthesis (1), (2) ...

You have to choose from four options, but only one corresponds to the volume modified according to the instructions. The other three are incorrect.

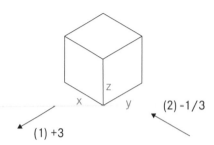

(2) -1/3

(1) +3

In this case, the first step implies adding three volumes of the same size to the starting volume. The second step implies reducing the resulting volume along the x-axis of a third.

Step (1): +3

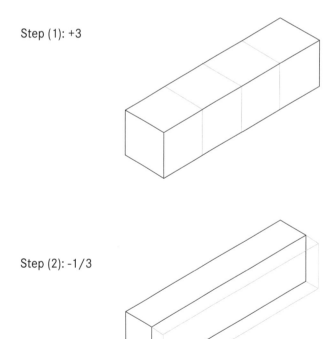

Step (2): -1/3

This exercise does not only foster the capacity to mentally conduct operations of addition and/or subtraction, but also to gain a sense for the proportion of volumes.
The proportions of the architectural references are approximations and taken from the whole volume.

Example

Try to solve this example by performing the two operations in sequence.

Warning: the target is not in the same scale as the four options.

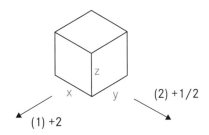

(2) +1/2

(1) +2

Baukontor Architekten, *Geschäftshaus am Schiffbauplatz,* Zurich, 2017

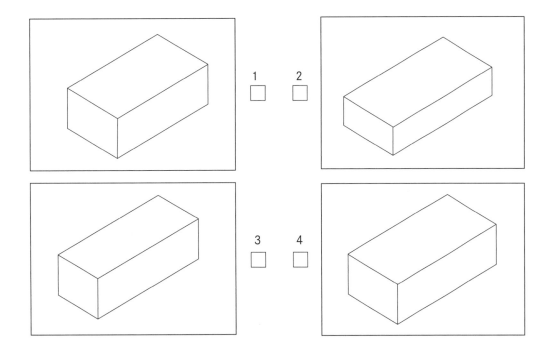

1 2

3 4

The correct answer is number 4. The volumes in 1, 2, and 3 have a difference of size either on the x, y, or z-axis.

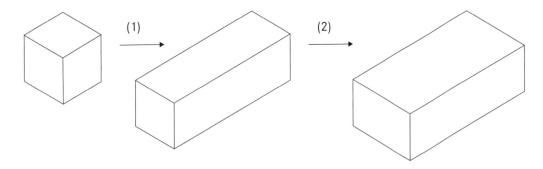

(1) (2)

Ingrid Wallberg, Alfred Roth, *Wallberg House,* Göteborg, 1935

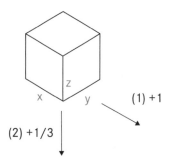

(1) +1

(2) +1/3

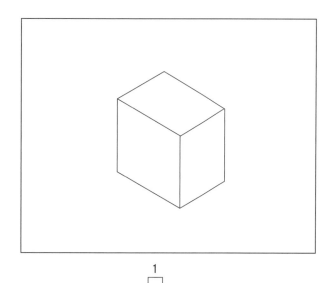

1

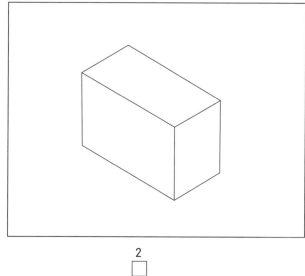

2

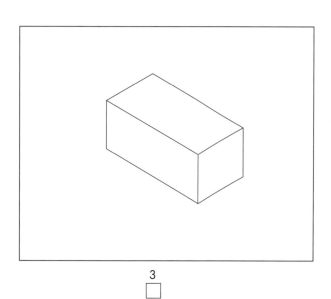

3

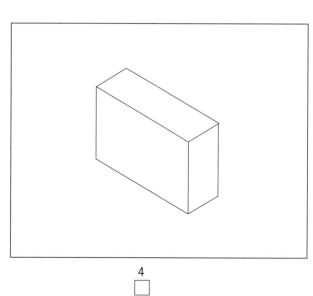

4

Theodor Fischer, *Parish Church,* Gaggstatt, 1905

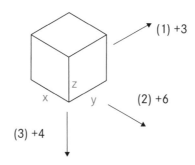

(1) +3

(2) +6

(3) +4

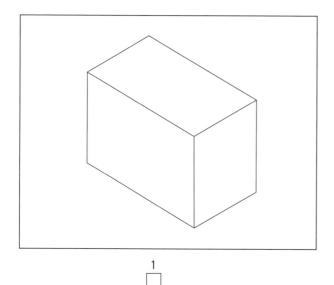

1

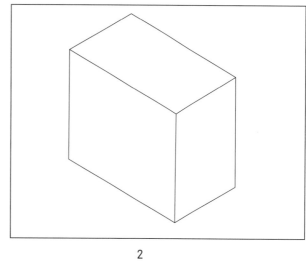

2

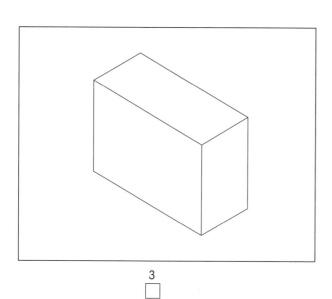

3

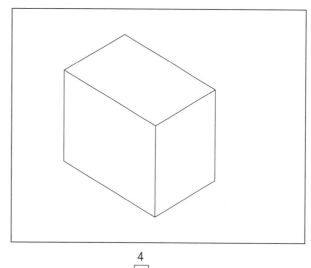

4

Le Corbusier, *Villa Savoye,* Poissy, 1931

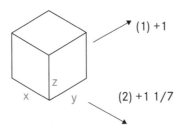

(1) +1

(2) +1 1/7

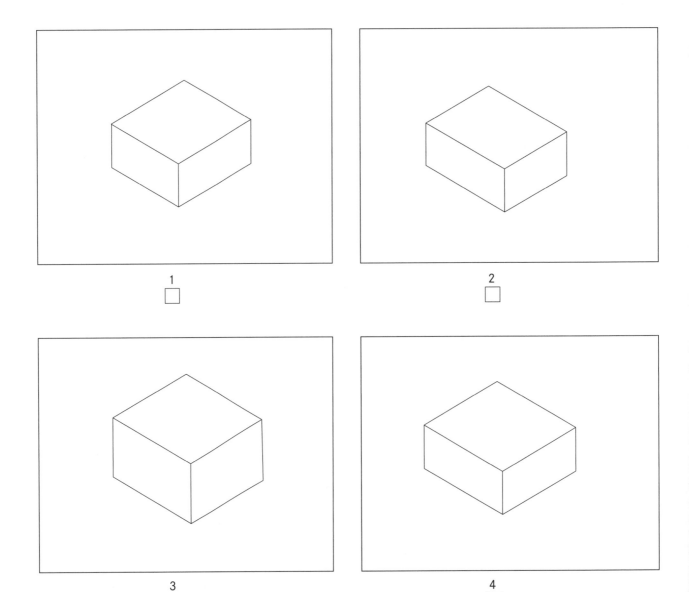

1

2

3

4

Peter Märkli, *Single Family House,* Grabs, 1995

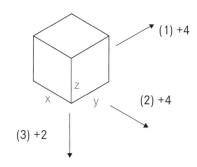

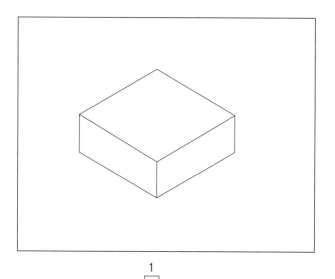

1 ☐

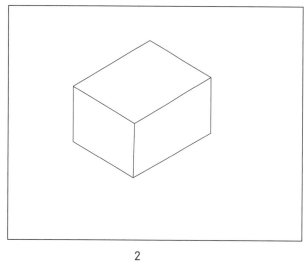

2 ☐

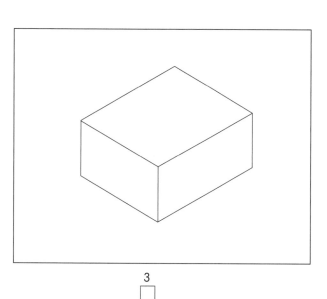

3 ☐

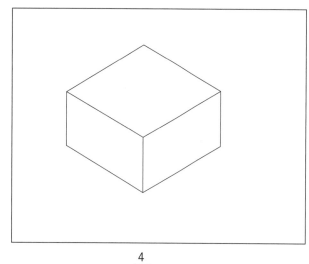

4 ☐

Leon Battista Alberti, *Arithmetic Proportions,* circa 1485

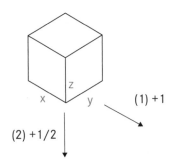

1 +1

(2) +1/2

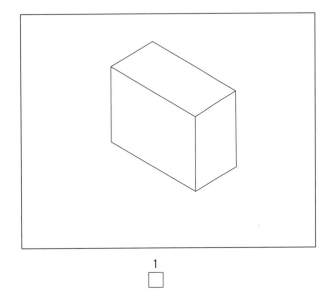

1

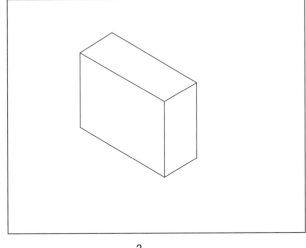

2

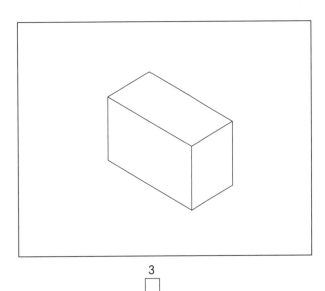

3

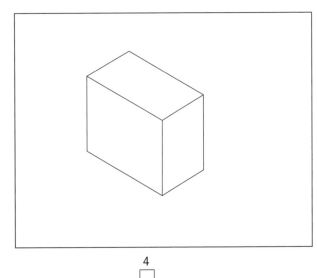

4

Leon Battista Alberti, *Geometric Proportions,* circa 1485

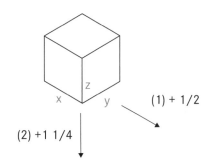

(1) + 1/2

(2) +1 1/4

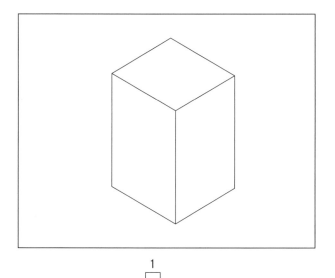

1

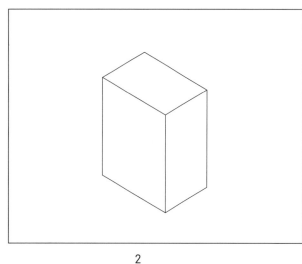

2

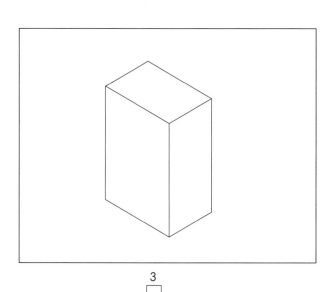

3

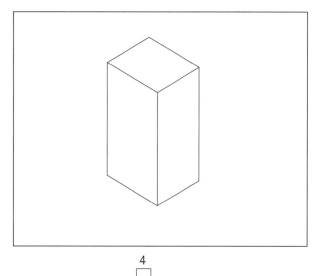

4

Francesco Giorgi, *S. Francesco della Vigna,* Venice, circa 1534

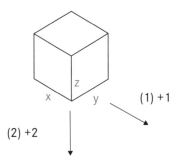

(1) +1

(2) +2

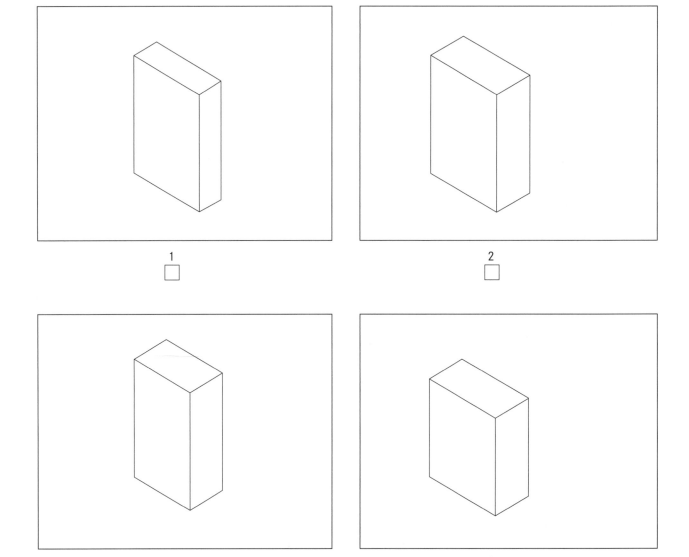

1

2

3

4

Paul Engelmann, Ludwig Wittgenstein, *House Wittgenstein,* Vienna, 1928

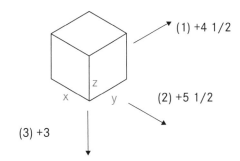

(1) +4 1/2

(2) +5 1/2

(3) +3

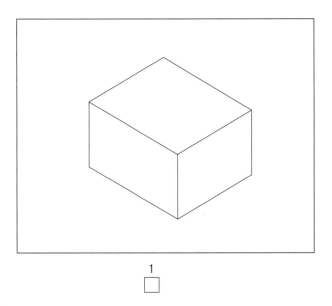

1

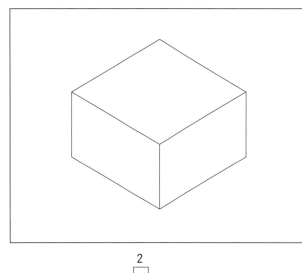

2

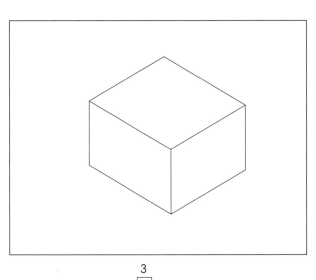

3

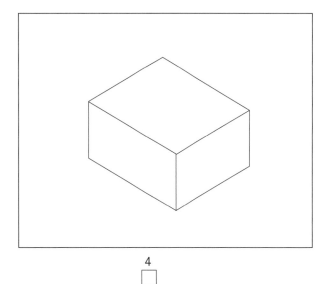

4

Tadao Ando, *Azuma House,* Osaka, 1976

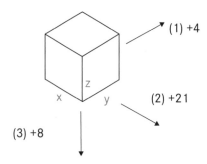

(1) +4

(2) +21

(3) +8

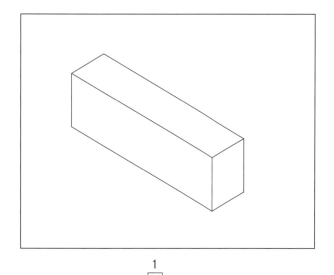

1 ☐

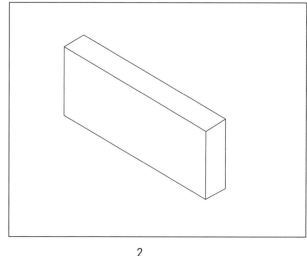

2 ☐

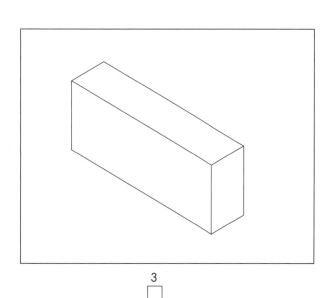

3 ☐

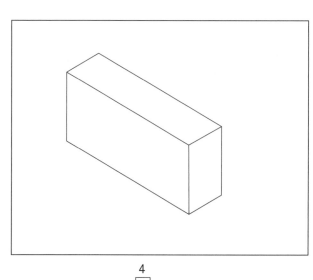

4 ☐

Eileen Gray, *E.1027,* Roquebrune-Cap-Martin, 1929

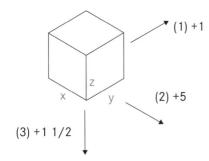

(1) +1

(2) +5

(3) +1 1/2

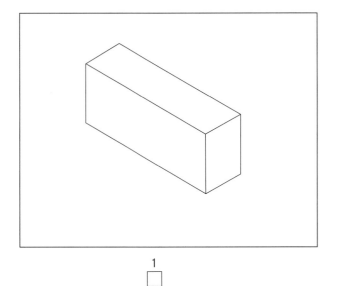

1

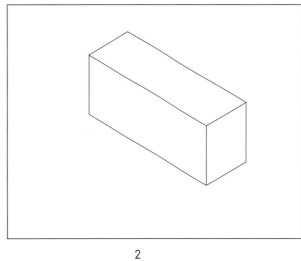

2

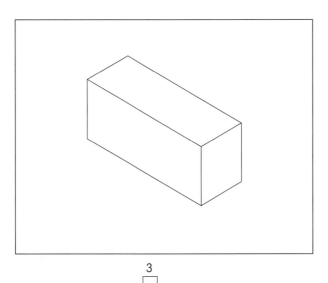

3

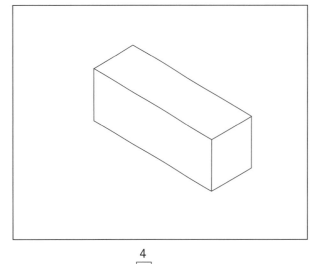

4

SANAA, *Zollverein School of Design,* Essen, 2006

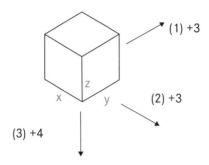

(1) +3

(2) +3

(3) +4

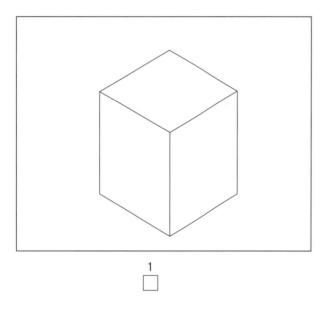

1

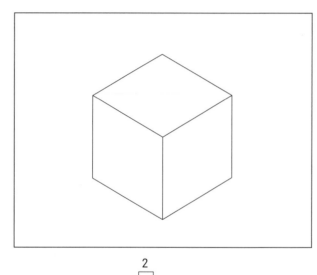

2

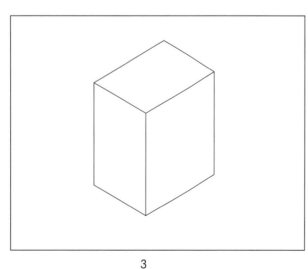

3

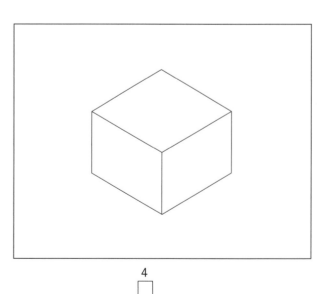

4

Peter and Alison Smithson, *Upper Lawn Pavilion,* Wiltshire, 1962

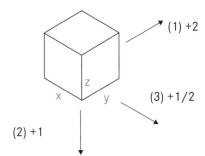

(1) +2

(3) +1/2

(2) +1

z

x   y

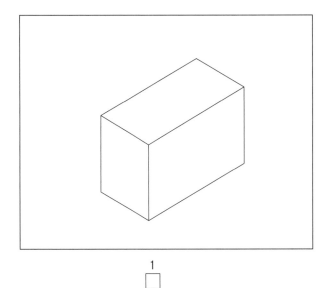

1

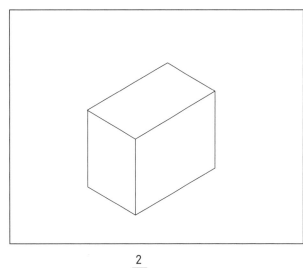

2

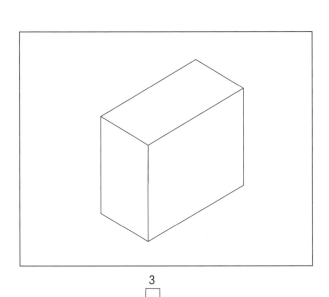

3

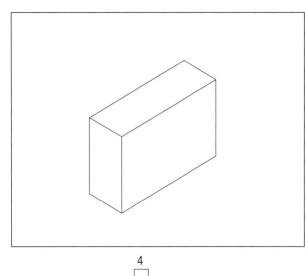

4

Philip Johnson, *Glass House,* New Canaan, 1962

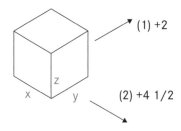

(1) +2

(2) +4 1/2

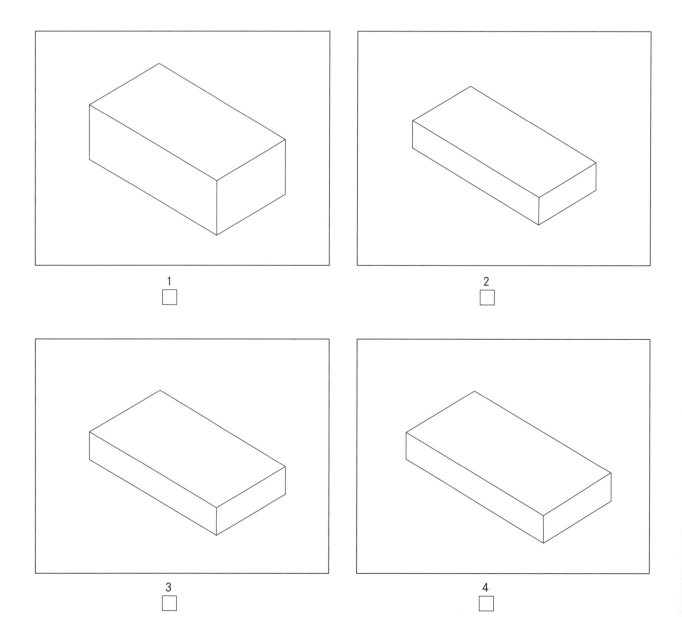

1

2

3

4

Mies van der Rohe, *Farnsworth House,* Illinois, 1951

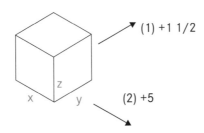

(1) +1 1/2

(2) +5

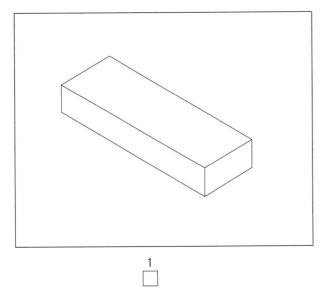

1

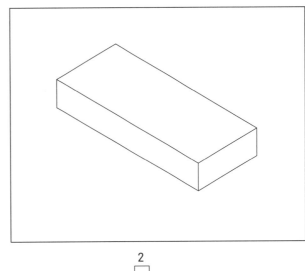

2

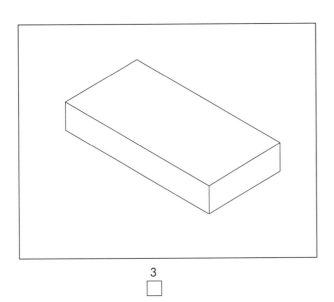

3

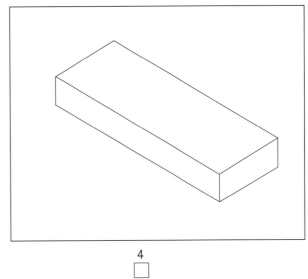

4

Kenzo Tange, *City Hall,* Kurashiki, 1960

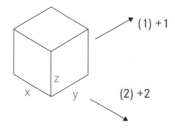

1

2

3

4

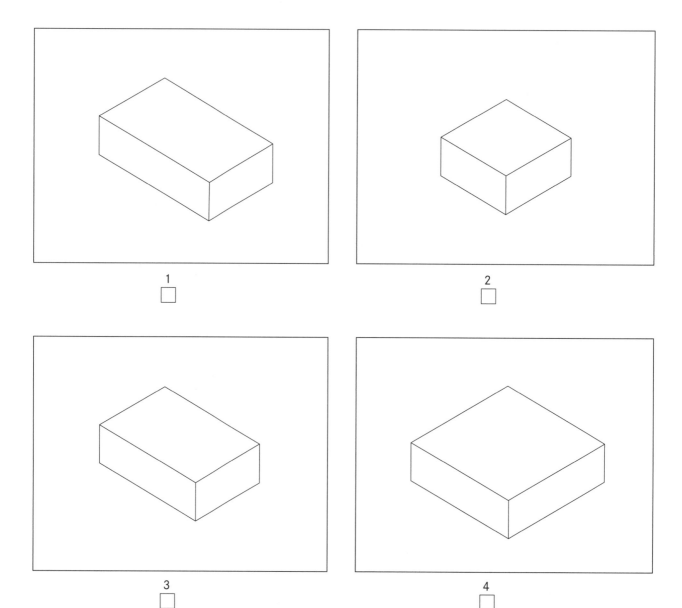

In this exercise, you have to cut through an architectural volume (full) and identify the corresponding section line. The section is then rotated from its original inclination to a vertical position, facing the viewer. You have to select the right answer from five options.

For every example there are always two images. The image on the left is a symbol of each building. The image on the right is the reference for making the cut. While the image on the left is more detailed and only representative, it can sometimes help to better understand the section.

William Morgan, *Goodloe Residence,* Florida, 1965

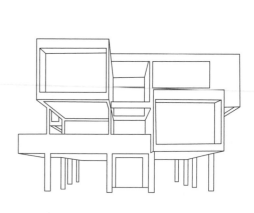
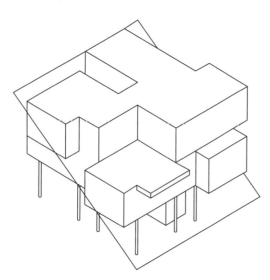

Which one of these five options is the correct one and corresponds to the surface resulting from cutting the volume with the inclined surface?

1 2 3 4 5

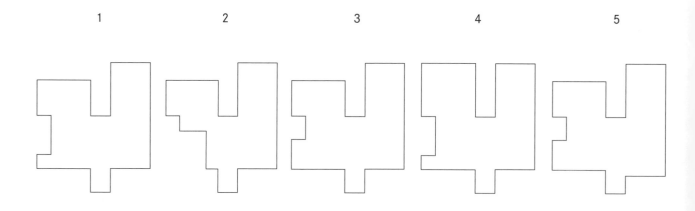

William Morgan, *Goodloe Residence,* Florida, 1965

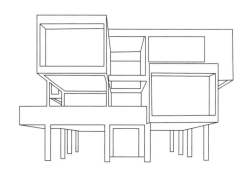

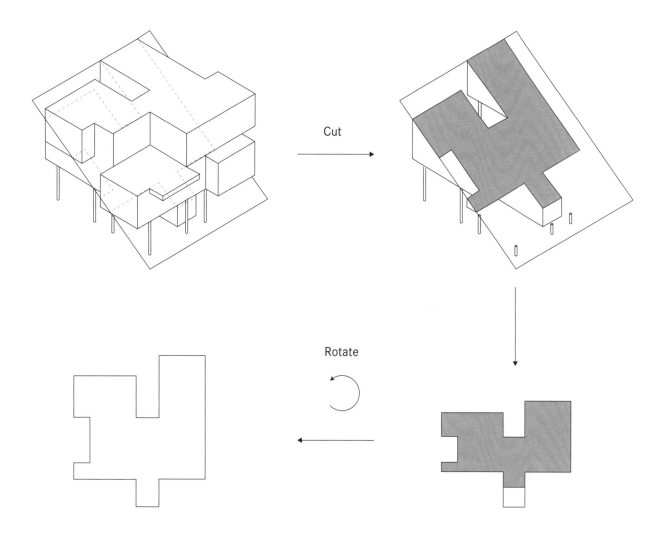

Cut

Rotate

The correct answer is option 1. Only this option corresponds
to the section of the volume along the inclined surface.

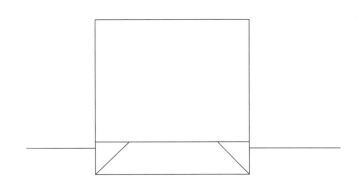

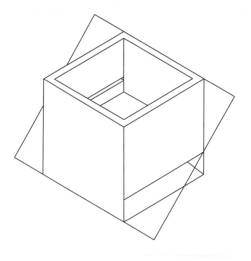

Aldo Rossi, *Monumento ai Caduti,* Cuneo, 1966

| 1 | 2 | 3 | 4 | 5 |

  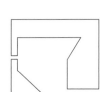 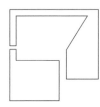

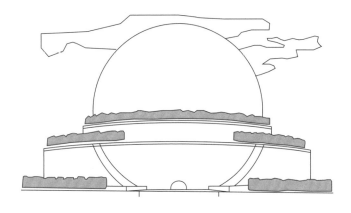

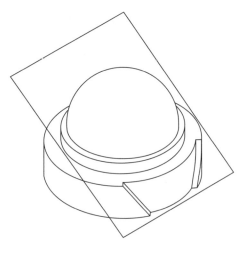

Étienne-Louis Boullée, *Cénotaphe à Newton,* 1784

| 1 | 2 | 3 | 4 | 5 |

   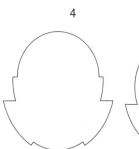 

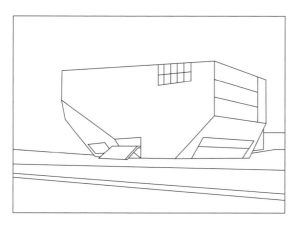

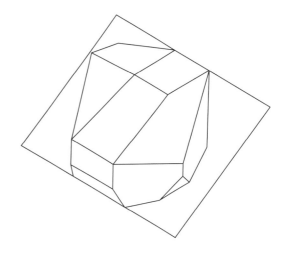

Rem Koolhaas, *Casa da Música,* Porto, 2005

1 2 3 4 5

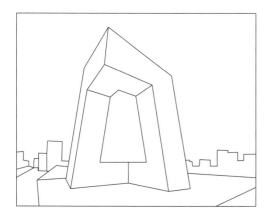

Rem Koolhaas, *CCTV - Headquarters,* Beijing, 2012

1 2 3 4 5

    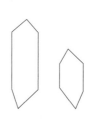 

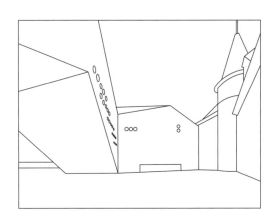 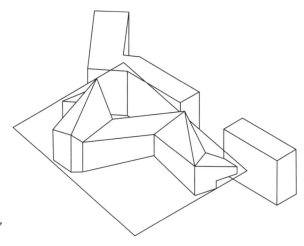

Christ & Gantenbein, *Swiss National Museum Extension,* Zurich, 2016

1   2   3   4   5

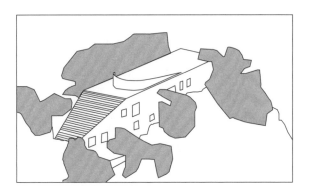 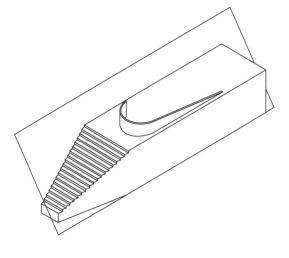

Curzio Malaparte, *Villa Malaparte,* Capri, 1940

1   2   3   4   5

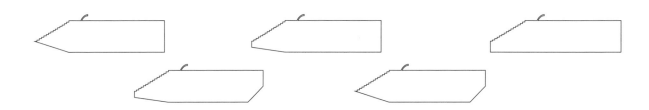

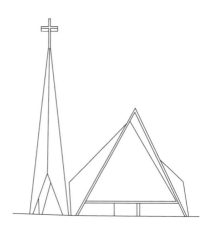

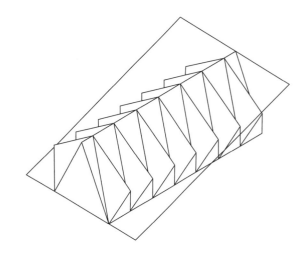

Paul R. Williams, *St. Viator Church,* Las Vegas, 1963

1	2	3	4	5
				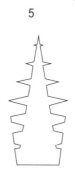

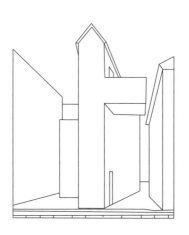

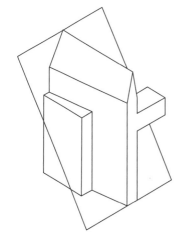

Go Hasegawa, *House in Shakujiikouen,* Tokyo, 2013

1	2	3	4	5

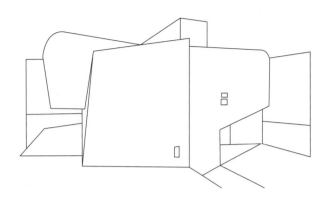

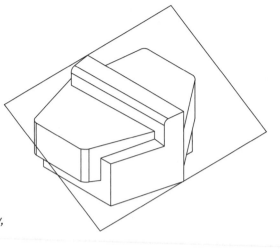

Claude Parent with Paul Virilio, *Église Sainte-Bernadette du Banlay,*
Nevers, 1966

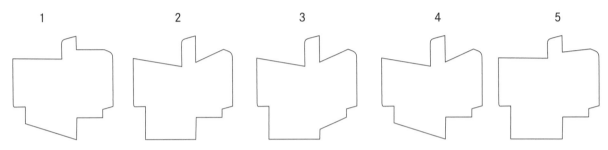

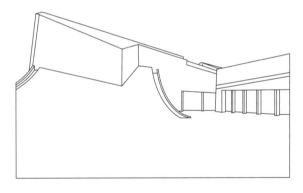

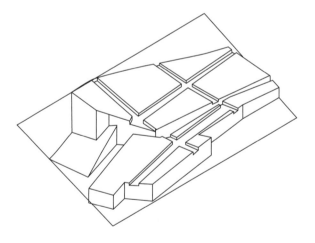

Peter Eisenman, *City of Culture of Galicia,* Santiago, 2011

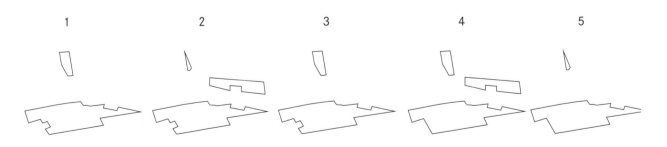

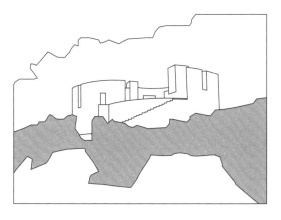
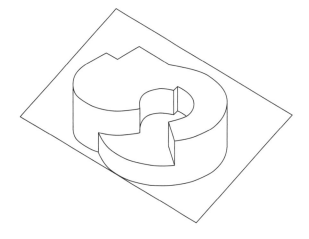

Cini Boeri, *Casa Rotonda,* Sassari, 1966–1967

1 2 3 4 5

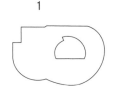
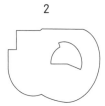
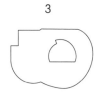
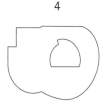
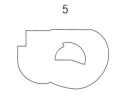

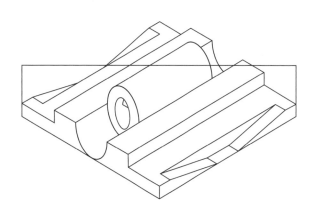

Claude-Nicolas Ledoux, *Maison de surveillants de la source de la Loue,* Chaux, 1804

1 2 3 4 5

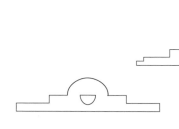

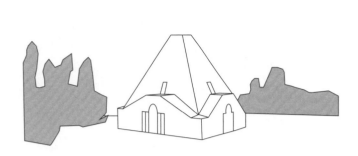
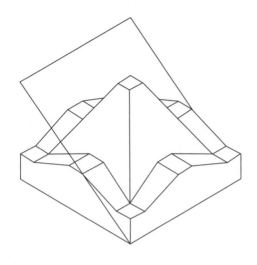

Claude-Nicolas Ledoux, *L'atelier des charbonniers,* Chaux, 1804

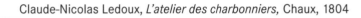

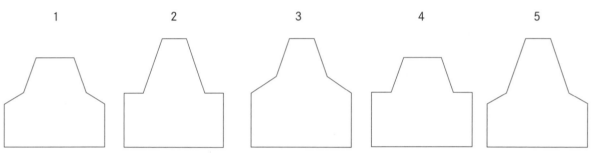

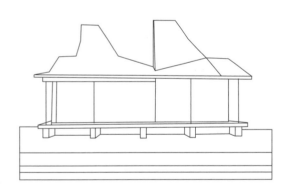
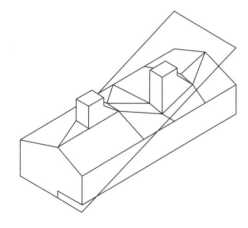

Atelier Bow-Wow, *Nora House,* Senndai, 2006

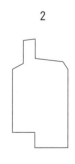
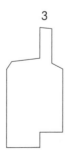

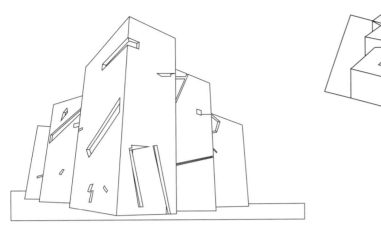

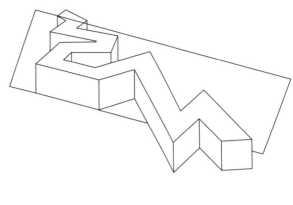

Daniel Libeskind, *Jewish Museum,* Berlin, 2001

1   2   3   4   5

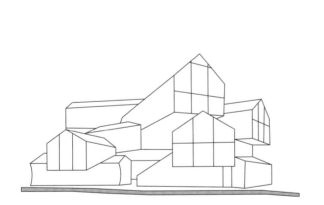

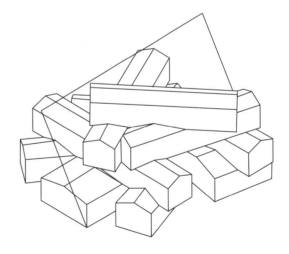

Herzog & de Meuron, *VitraHaus,* Weil am Rhein, 2010

1   2   3   4   5

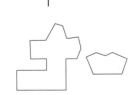
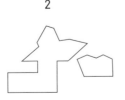
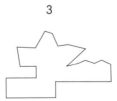
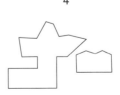

SOLUTIONS

Urban Layout Test

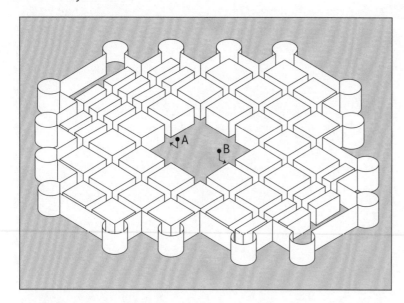

A [4]   B [3]

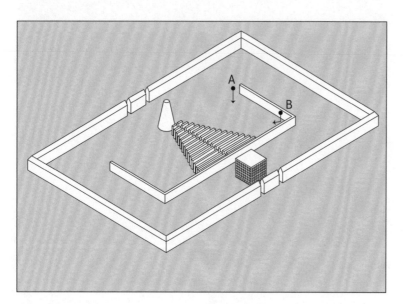

A [3]   B [1]

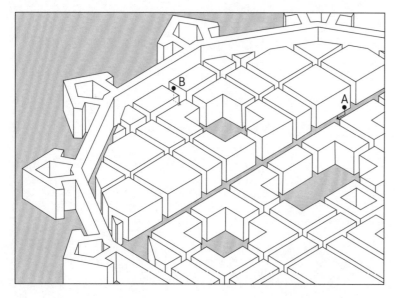

A [3]   B [1]

Urban Layout Test

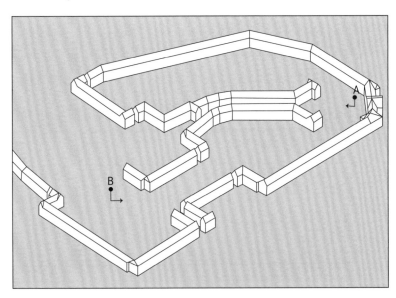

A [1]   B [4]

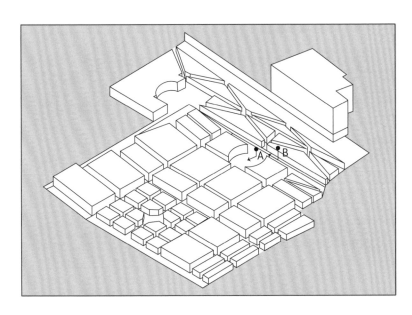

A [1]   B [2]

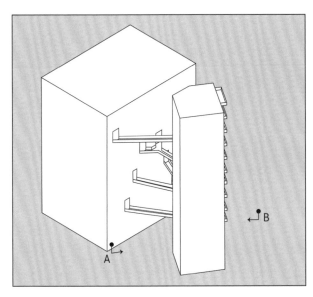

A [2]   B [3]

Urban Layout Test

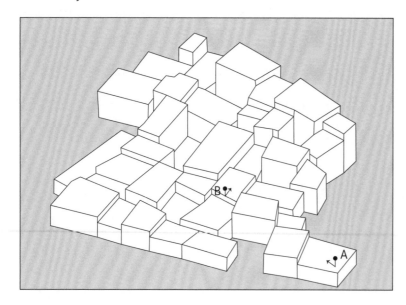

A [3]   B [2]

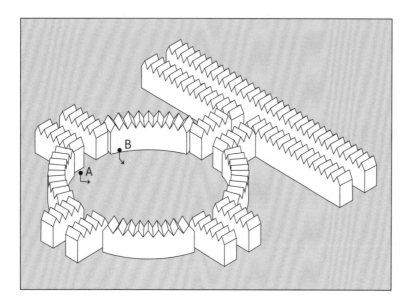

A [4]   B [2]

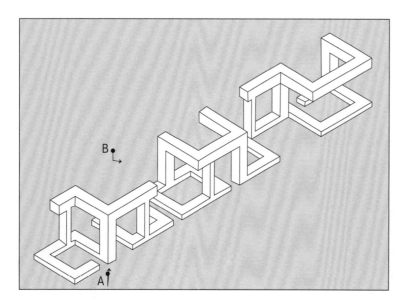

A [2]   B [1]

Urban Layout Test

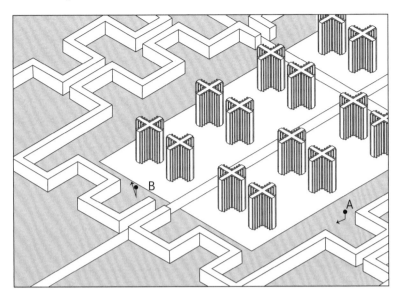

A [1]   B [3]

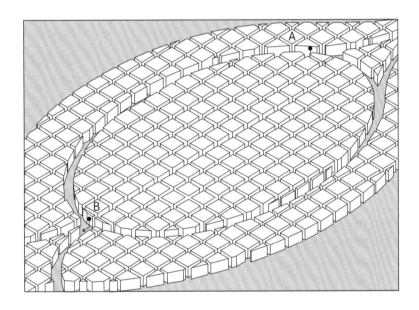

A [2]   B [1]

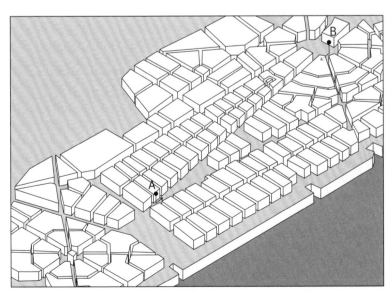

A [1]   B [3]

Urban Layout Test

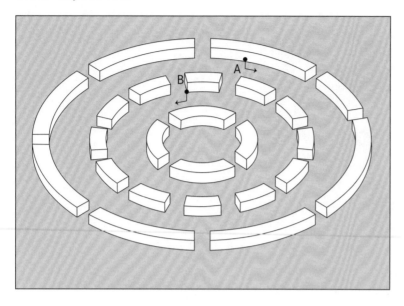

A [4]   B [3]

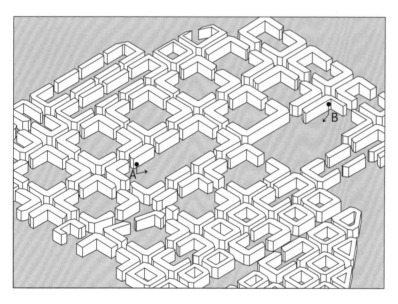

A [1]   B [2]

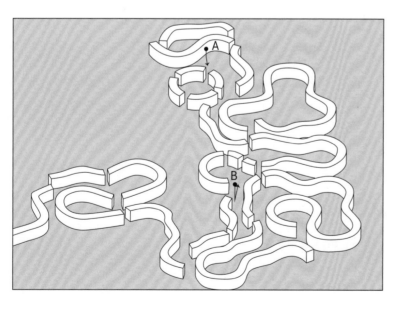

A [2]   B [4]

Indoor Perspective Test

		Solution
1	Robert Venturi, Lieb House, New Jersey, 1967	1
2	Valerio Olgiati, School in Paspels, Domleschg, 1998	4
3	Gunnar Asplund, Summer house, Stennäs, 1937	4
4	Peter Zumthor, Thermen Vals, Vals, 1998	2
5	Álvaro Siza, Saint-Jacques-de-la-Lande, Rennes, 2018	1
6	Myron Goldfinger, Goldfinger House, Waccabuc, NY, 1970	3
7	Valerio Olgiati, Villa Além, Portugal, 2014	2
8	Louis Kahn, Jewish Community Center, New Jersey, 1959	1
9	Rem Koolhaas, CCTV – Headquarters, Beijing, 2012	4
10	Kazuo Shinohara, Tanikawa House, 1974	3
11	Frank Gehry, Guest House Winton, Minnesota, 1987	4
12	Agustín Hernández, Architectural Office, Mexico City, 1975	2
13	Iseppi-Kurath, Viamala Gas Station, Thusis, 2008	3
14	Toyo Ito, Tama Art University library, Tokyo, 2007	1
15	Pezo von Ellrichshausen, Svara Pavilion, Venice, 2016	4

Packing Test

MVRDV, *Silodam*, Amsterdam, 2003

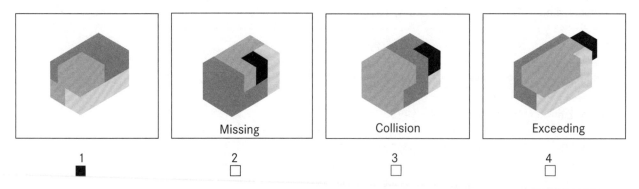

1	2	3	4
■	□	□	□

Mario Botta, *Casa Medici,* Stabio, 1982

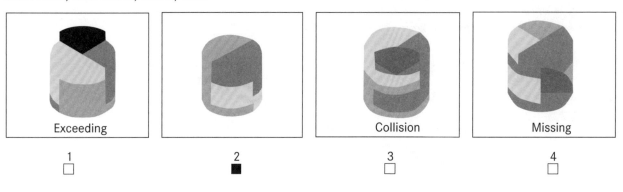

1	2	3	4
□	■	□	□

Kazuyo Sejima, *Kitagata Apartment Building,* Gifu, 2000

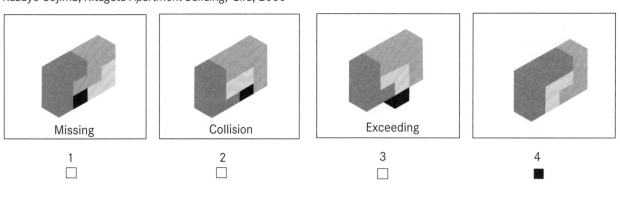

1	2	3	4
□	□	□	■

Adolf Loos, *House Tristan Tzara,* Paris, 1926

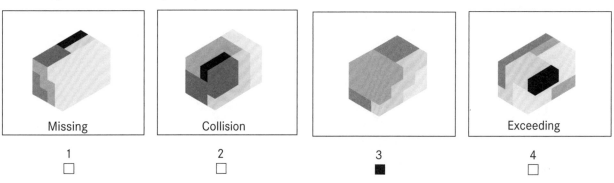

1	2	3	4
□	□	■	□

Packing Test

Walter Gropius, Fred Forbàt, *Baukasten im Grossen,* Dessau, 1923

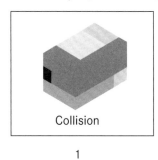
Collision

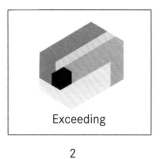
Exceeding

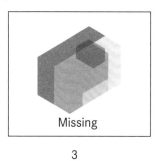
Missing

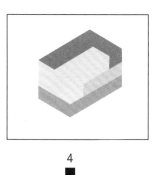

1	2	3	4
☐	☐	☐	■

Sou Fujimoto, *Final Wooden House,* Kumamoto, 2006

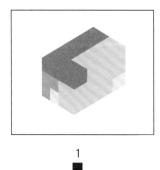

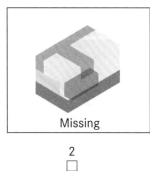
Missing

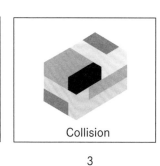
Collision

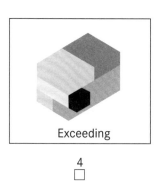
Exceeding

1	2	3	4
■	☐	☐	☐

Claude Parent/Paul Virilio, *Maison Mariotti,* Saint-Germain-en-Laye, 1970

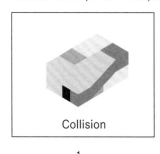
Collision

Missing

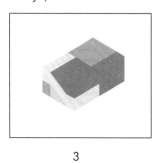

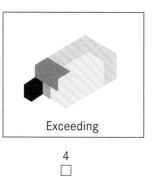
Exceeding

1	2	3	4
☐	☐	■	☐

Raimund Abraham, *House for Musicians,* Hombroich, 1999

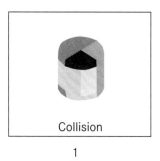
Collision

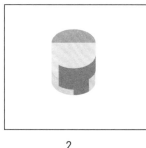

Missing

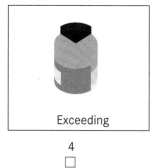
Exceeding

1	2	3	4
☐	■	☐	☐

Packing Test

HHF/BIG, *Puzzle House,* Denmark, 2019

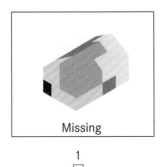

Missing

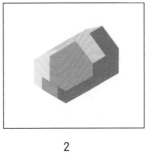

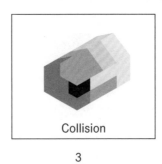

Collision

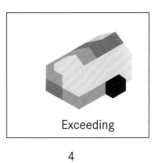

Exceeding

1	2	3	4
☐	■	☐	☐

Paul and Blanche Mahlberg/Bruno Taut, *Dandanah*, 1920

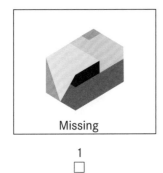

Missing

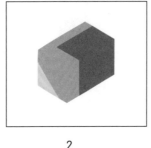

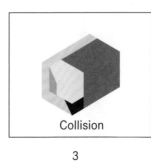

Collision

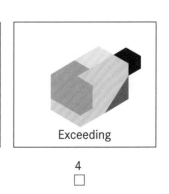

Exceeding

1	2	3	4
☐	■	☐	☐

Daniel Libeskind, *V & A Museum Extension,* London, 2002

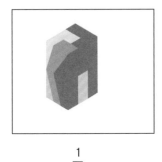

Missing

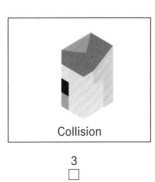

Collision

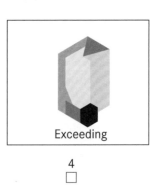

Exceeding

1	2	3	4
■	☐	☐	☐

Rem Koolhaas, *Dutch Embassy,* Berlin, 2004

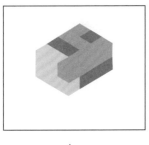

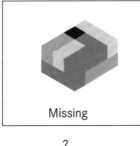

Missing

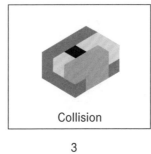

Collision

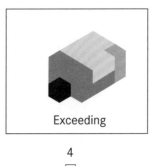

Exceeding

1	2	3	4
■	☐	☐	☐

Packing Test

Ben van Berkel, *Möbius House,* Het Gooi, 1998

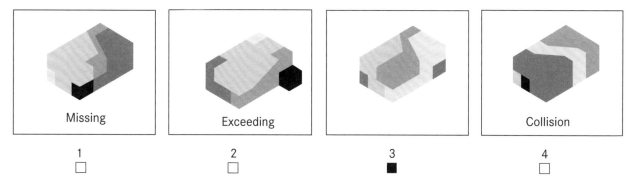

Missing	Exceeding		Collision
1	2	3	4
☐	☐	■	☐

Le Corbusier, *Unité d'habitation,* Marseille, 1952

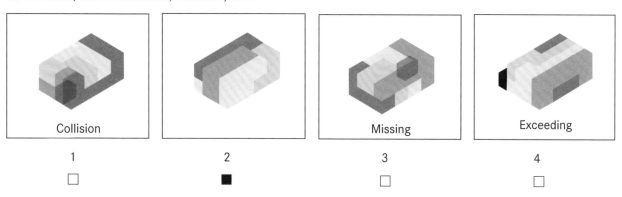

Collision		Missing	Exceeding
1	2	3	4
☐	■	☐	☐

Fuhriman & Hächler, *Haus Eva Presenhuber,* Vnà, 2017

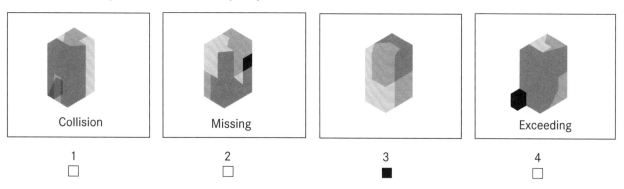

Collision	Missing		Exceeding
1	2	3	4
☐	☐	■	☐

Mental Construction Test

Ingrid Wallberg, Alfred Roth, *Wallberg House*,
Göteborg, 1935

2 ■

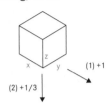

(1) +1

(2) +1/3

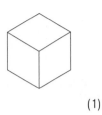

(1)

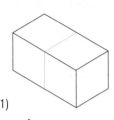

(2)

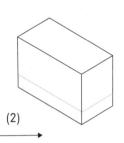

Theodor Fischer, *Evangelische Pfarrkirche
zum heiligen Kreuz,* Gaggstatt, 1905

1 ■

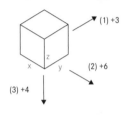

(1) +3

(2) +6

(3) +4

(1)

(2)

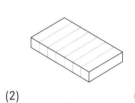

(3)

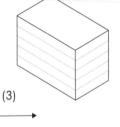

Le Corbusier, *Villa Savoye,* Poissy, 1931

4 ■

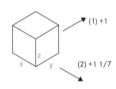

(1) +1

(2) +1 1/7

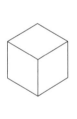

(1)

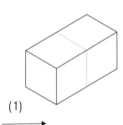

(2)

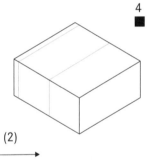

Peter Märkli, *Single Family House,* Grabs, 1995

4 ■

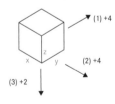

(1) +4

(2) +4

(3) +2

(1)

(2)

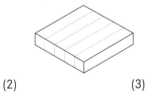

(3)

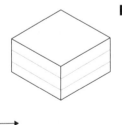

Leon Battista Alberti, *Arithmetic Proportions,*
circa 1485

1 ■

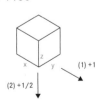

(1) +1

(2) +1/2

(1)

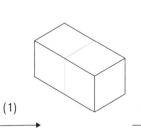

(2)

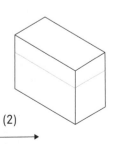

Mental Construction Test

Leon Battista Alberti, *Geometric Proportions*,
circa 1485

3

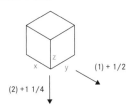

(1) + 1/2

(2) +1 1/4

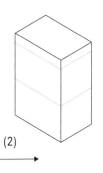

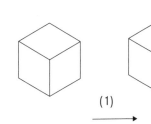

(1)

(2)

Francesco Giorgi, *S. Francesco della Vigna,*
Venice, circa 1534

2

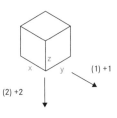

(1) +1

(2) +2

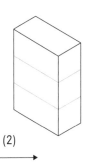

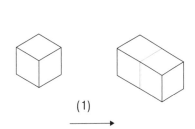

(1)

(2)

Paul Engelmann, Ludwig Wittgenstein,
House Wittgenstein, Vienna, 1928

1

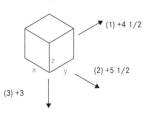

(1) +4 1/2

(2) +5 1/2

(3) +3

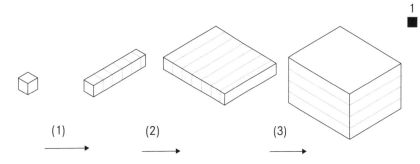

(1)

(2)

(3)

Tadao Ando, *Azuma House,*
Osaka, 1976

3

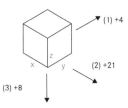

(1) +4

(2) +21

(3) +8

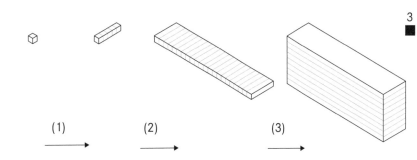

(1)

(2)

(3)

Eileen Gray, *E.1027,* Roquebrune-Cap-Martin,
1929

2

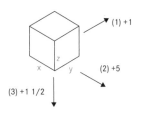

(1) +1

(2) +5

(3) +1 1/2

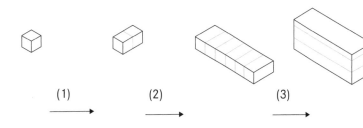

(1)

(2)

(3)

Mental Construction Test

SANAA, *Zollverein School of Design*,
Essen, 2006

1
■

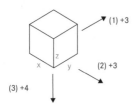

      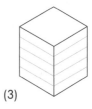

(1) →   (2) →   (3) →

Peter and Alison Smithson, *Upper Lawn
Pavilion*, Wiltshire, 1962

1
■

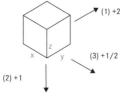

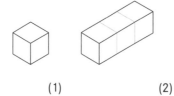 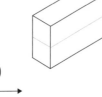 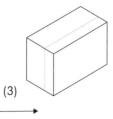

(1) →   (2) →   (3) →

Philip Johnson, *Glass House*,
New Canaan, 1949

3
■

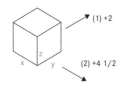

    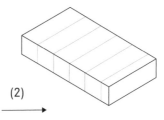

(1) →   (2) →

Mies van der Rohe, *Farnsworth House*,
Illinois, 1951

2
■

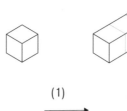 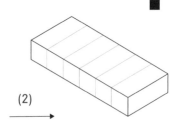

(1) →   (2) →

Kenzo Tange, *City Hall*,
Kurashiki, 1960

3
■

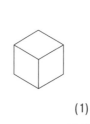 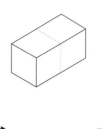 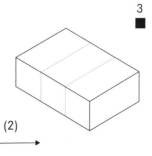

(1) →   (2) →

Mental Cutting Test, Architecture

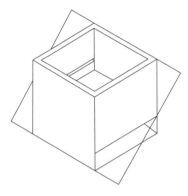 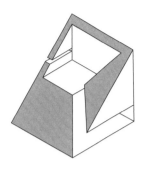 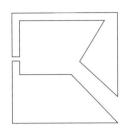

Aldo Rossi, *Monumento ai Caduti,* Cuneo, 1966

1

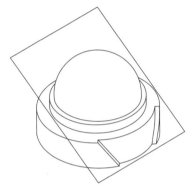 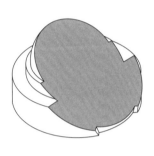 

Étienne-Louis Boullée, *Cénotaphe à Newton,* 1784

3

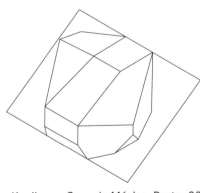 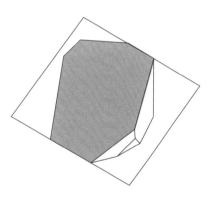 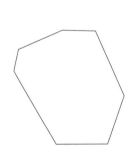

Rem Koolhaas, *Casa da Música,* Porto, 2005

1

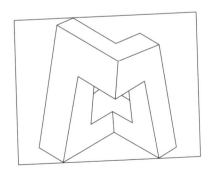 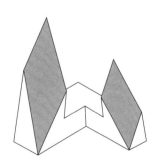 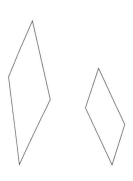

Rem Koolhaas, *CCTV – Headquarters,* Beijing, 2012

3

Mental Cutting Test, Architecture

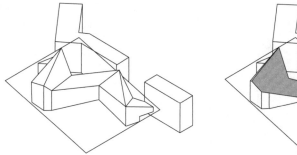 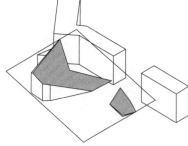 

Christ & Gantenbein, *Swiss National Museum Extension,* Zurich, 2016

3

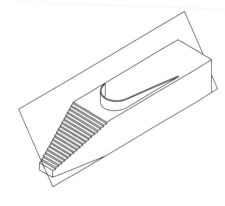 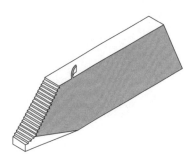 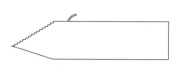

Curzio Malaparte, *Villa Malaparte,* Capri, 1940

1

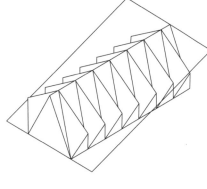 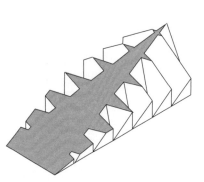 

Paul R. Williams, *St. Viator Church,* Las Vegas, 1963

5

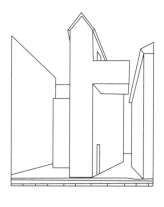 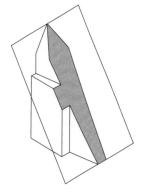 

Go Hasegawa, *House in Shakujiikouen,* Tokyo, 2013

2

Mental Cutting Test, Architecture

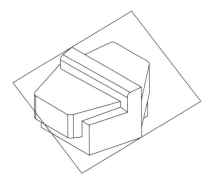  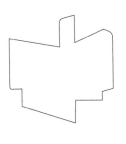

Claude Parent with Paul Virilio, *Église Sainte-Bernadette du Banlay,* Nevers, 1966   4

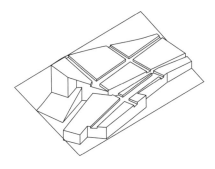 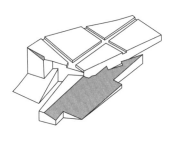 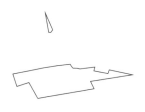

Peter Eisenman, *City of Culture of Galicia,* Santiago, 2011   5

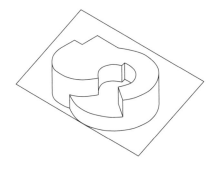 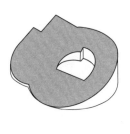 

Cini Boeri, *Casa Rotonda,* Sassari, 1966–1967   4

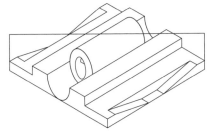 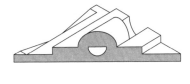 

Claude-Nicolas Ledoux, *Maison de surveillants de la source de la Loue,* Chaux, 1804   5

Mental Cutting Test, Architecture

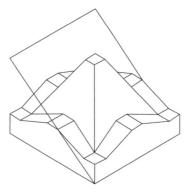 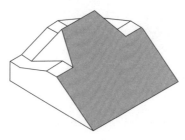 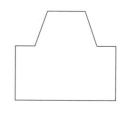

Claude-Nicolas Ledoux, *L'atelier des charbonniers,* Chaux, 1804

4

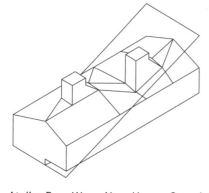 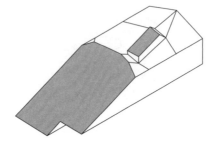 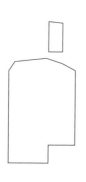

Atelier Bow-Wow, *Nora House,* Senndai, 2006

3

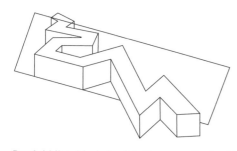 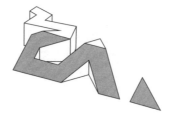 

Daniel Libeskind, *Jewish Museum,* Berlin, 2001

3

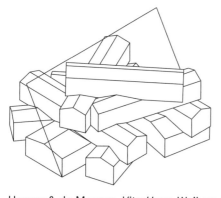 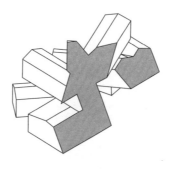 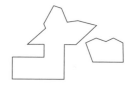

Herzog & de Meuron, *VitraHaus,* Weil am Rhein, 2010

2

ACKNOWLEDGEMENTS

If interdisciplinary research with architects is possible at all, it is because of very patient scientists, as was the case here. Without the patience and knowledge of Dr. Michal Berkowitz, Prof. Dr. Christoph Hölscher, Prof. Dr. Elsbeth Stern, and Dr. Beatrix Emo, this project would not have been possible. Interdisciplinary research is a painful path full of misunderstanding and suspicion for sometimes incomprehensible disciplinary singularities. Only when one can engage with these aspects is communication and exchange possible.

Neither would the project have been possible without the help of so many others. First of all, we would like to thank a series of experts who accompanied the project: Ruth Conroy Dalton, Dafna Fischer Gewirtzman, Peter Holgate, Thomas Shipley, Margaret Tarampi, and David Uttal. Beyond these direct influences, Nora N. Newcombe and Mary Hegarty should be mentioned as fundamental references and inspirations for anybody working on spatial abilities.

We would also like to thank the design professors who granted us access to their students: François Charbonnet, Andreas Deplazes, Dieter Dietz, Harry Gugger, Patrick Heiz, Johannes Käferstein, Cornelie Leopold, Marco Merz, Urs Primas, Wolfgang Rossbauer, Lando Rossmaier, Detlef Schulz, Annette Spiro, Christina Schumacher, Peter Staub, and Toni Wirth.

A great thanks is also extended to Nuno De Matos Ferreira for his valuable assistance in carrying out the various phases of this project. Many thanks also to Ivo Costa and Alexandra Vier Gehrmann, who drew most of the street view test items.

Many thanks also to our colleagues at ZHAW and ETH for the enriching and sometimes heated discussions and for testing the material of our project: Anke Domschky, Oya Atalay Franck, Regula Iseli, Peter Jenny, Stefan Kurath, Philipp Koch, Simon Mühlebach, Yesol Park, Urs Primas, Victor Shinazi, Holger Schurk, Rainer Schützeichel, Nina Sommer, Tyler Thrash, Martin Tschanz, Andrea Wäger, Matthew Wells, Toni Winiger, and in particular Andreas Jud and Andreas Kalpakci.

Many thanks also to Lindsay Blair Howe for her work on the "different languages" of this book.

Last but not least, this project was financed by a Sinergia Grant from the Swiss National Science Foundation, without which it would never have been possible.

AUTHORS

MICHAL BERKOWITZ is a postdoctoral researcher at the Chair for Research on Learning and Instruction at the ETH Zurich. She studied psychology at Tel-Aviv University and began her career in clinical psychology. She later moved on to research in cognitive psychology, and obtained her doctoral degree in 2017 at the Chair for Research on Learning and Instruction at the ETH Zurich. Her doctoral research focused on cognitive predictors of advanced STEM achievements, particularly in math-intensive domains. Her research interests include the role of spatial ability in STEM learning, mathematical thinking and learning, and the interplay between working memory, intelligence, and learning.

TERESA CHEUNG, ALICE EPFL, is an architect who graduated from the AA in London in 2006 and has practiced architecture in New York, Hong Kong, London, and in Switzerland. She has been a member of the ALICE team from 2010 to 2015 where she taught both first year and diploma students alongside developing pedagogical instruments for the first-year program. Returning as a studio director to ALICE in 2018, Cheung is now the Academic Head of ALICE y1. She is also a curator at Eye on Science, an association fostering public discourse on science through art and film.

DIETER DIETZ, ALICE EPFL. Educated at the ETH (Arch. Degree 1991), he also studied at the Cooper Union in New York with Diller/Scofidio. Since 2006, he has been Associate Professor for Architectural Design at EPFL, director of the ALICE laboratory in the ENAC faculty. He collaborates with the ALICE team on research projects at diverse scales.

BEATRIX EMO is a practicing architect, and director of Spatialist Arch. She holds a PhD from the Bartlett School of Architecture, in which she explored how individuals experience urban spaces. She is a postdoctoral researcher at the Chair of Cognitive Science, an interdisciplinary group where she leads the focus on how people interact with the environment. Her interests lie in urban design, space syntax and spatial cognition, conducting experiments in real and virtual environments. Emo is recipient of the ETH Career Seed Grant for the project "Human Centered Urban Design: Analyzing pedestrians' perceived density of public space." Emo is guest lecturer at the Institute for the History and Theory of Architecture (gta), ETH Zurich, at the Bartlett School of Architecture, UCL, and at the Faculty of Architecture (fatuk), Technical University Kaiserslautern.

ANDRI GERBER is an architectural and planning historian and an urban metaphorologist. He studied architecture at the ETH Zurich and was a project architect and project manager for Peter Eisenman in New York. In 2008, he received his doctorate from the ETH Zurich, for which he was awarded the ETH Medal. From 2008 to 2011 he was a visiting and associate professor at the *Ecole spéciale d'architecture* in Paris. Since 2011, he has been a lecturer and since 2017 professor in urban planning history at the Zurich University of Applied Sciences (ZHAW). He completed his habilitation in 2016 at the ETHZ's gta Institute, funded by an SNSF Ambizione Scholarship. Gerber is private lecturer at the ETHZ since August 2017. His research interest focuses on space and metaphors, specifically from a cognitive perspective.

PETER HOLGATE studied architecture at the Universities of Liverpool and Oregon, and practiced in London, San Francisco, Frankfurt, and Newcastle upon Tyne. Formerly a Director for FaulknerBrowns Architects, he was responsible for the delivery of several award-winning projects. He has taught architecture at Northumbria University since 2005, receiving his doctorate in education in 2016, and he currently acts as Associate Professor of Architecture and Departmental Director of Learning and Teaching. He is a Senior Fellow and Academic Associate of the Higher Education Academy, a member of the Association of Architectural Educators, an executive committee member of the Assessment in Higher Education network, and an external examiner for the Architects Registration Board, Robert Gordon, Bath and VIA Universities.

CHRISTOPH HÖLSCHER is Full Professor of Cognitive Science in the D-GESS at the ETH Zurich since 2013, with an emphasis on Applied Cognitive Science. Since 2016, Hölscher has been a Principal Investigator at the Singapore ETH Center (SEC) Future Cities Laboratory, heading a research group on "Cognition, Perception and Behavior in Urban Environments." He holds a PhD in Psychology from University of Freiburg, served as honorary senior research fellow at UCL, Bartlett School of Architecture, and as a visiting Professor at Northumbria University Newcastle. Hölscher has several years of industry experience in Human-Computer Interaction and usability consulting. The core mission of his research groups in Zurich and Singapore is to unravel the complex interaction of humans and their physical, technical, and social environment with an emphasis on cognitive processes and task-oriented behavior.

LUCÍA JALÓN OYARZUN, ALICE EPFL. An architect and researcher, she graduated from the ETSAM School of Architecture of Madrid, where she received her PhD in 2017. She is Head of Research at ALICE at the EPFL, and Director for Academic Affairs at Escuela SUR, a postgraduate school of arts in Madrid.

STEFAN KURATH is an architect and urbanist. He studied architecture in Switzerland and the Netherlands. In 2011, he received his doctorate (summa cum laude) from the HCU in Hamburg. Since 2012, he has been professor for architecture and urban design at the Zurich University of Applied Sciences (ZHAW). Next to the academy, he runs his own office in Zurich and Grison. His interests focus on the history of the built environment, urban morphology, public space, and the relationship between the architecture of the city and society.

JULIEN LAFONTAINE CARBONI, ALICE EPFL. He studied at Paris-Malaquais (ENSAPM, MSc Arch 2017), and in Clermont-Ferrand (ENSACF). He currently pursues his PhD at ALICE. He explores the history of the city thanks to the concept of Protofiguration. Acts and gestures of settlements in plural civilization are studied, as diagrams, potential and operational geometries of transindividuation.

CORNELIE LEOPOLD teaches and researches in the field of architectural geometry at FATUK, TU Kaiserslautern, Germany, in the position as academic director and head of the section Descriptive Geometry and Perspective. She received her degree in mathematics, philosophy and German philology at Stuttgart University, with a specialization in geometry, aesthetics, and philosophy of science. She is member of the editorial board of the *Nexus Network Journal*, the *Journal for Geometry and Graphics* and of the scientific committee of the Journal *Diségno*. She is author and editor of several books, and participated with lectures and reviews in numerous international conferences, journals, and book series. In 2017, she was visiting professor at the Università Iuav di Venezia. Her research interests are: architectural geometry and design, visualization of architecture, development of spatial visualization abilities, and the philosophical background of architecture.

THOMAS F. SHIPLEY is a professor of psychology in the area of cognitive science. He studied psychology at the University of Pennsylvania. In 1988, he received his doctorate from the University of Pennsylvania.

From 1988 to 1991 he was a post-doctoral fellow at Swarthmore College and from 1991 to 1993 an assistant professor at the University of Georgia, Athens. Since 1993, he has been an assistant professor and since 2018, professor at Temple University in Philadelphia. His early research focused on object and event perception, and his current interest centers on the role of spatial reasoning in learning and practice in the geosciences.

NOAH H. SHIPLEY is a fourth-year student at the Rhode Island School of Design and is currently studying architecture with a focus on nature-culture-sustainability studies. His interests include landscapes and their representations, projective geometry, and growable design.

DETLEF SCHULZ received his master's degree in Architecture in 1991 at the ETH Zurich under Prof. Hans Kollhoff's professorship. Between 1991 and 2000 he was employed at Bétrix & Consolascio (Erlenbach), Burgdorf & Burren (Zurich) and Meili & Peter (Zurich). From 2000 to 2003 he established a joint business with Philipp Esch in Zurich and between 2003 and 2006 created his own company in Zurich. In 2006 he formed the company GFA Gruppe für Architektur Ltd. with Barbara Burren and Ilinca Manaila. From 2001 to 2008 he was diploma assistantship of Prof. Adrian Meyer at ETH Zurich. Since 2007, he has been lecturer in the faculties of design and construction at Zurich University of Applied Sciences (Winterthur) and a member of the BSA since 2006.

ELSBETH STERN is a cognitive psychologist with a focus on STEM learning at various age levels. As a professor for learning and instruction at the ETH Zurich, she is heading the teacher education program. In more than 100 papers and several books she has focused on the interaction between individual preconditions and instructional support of learning.

DAVID UTTAL is professor of education and psychology at Northwestern University. He is also the Northwestern University Dan Linzer Fellow for developmental science, an honor given to the faculty to recognize leadership in transdisciplinary research. He is the recipient of the 2014 George Miller Award for the best paper in general psychology from the American Psychological Association and the 2016 Research Award from the *Journal of Geography*. He was the PI of two IES-funded research grants and an IES Training Grant. He is Director of the Spatial Intelligence and Learning Center. He is the author of approximately 100 articles and book chapters, many of which have been published in leading journals such as *Psychological Bulletin* and *Child Development*. His research focuses on the development of spatial cognition in children, through experiments exploring the comprehension of concrete objects as symbols, and comprehension and memory for spatial objects depicted on maps. In addition, Uttal studies the relationship between spatial skills and STEM achievement and attainment, attempting to go beyond correlations to understand causal mechanisms.

IMAGE COPYRIGHTS

Andri Gerber

Fig. 1 Gropius, Walter. *Scope of Total Architecture*. London: Allen & Unwin, 1956.

Fig. 2 Schubert, Otto. *Optik in Architektur und Städtebau*. Berlin: Mann, 1965, 17.

Fig. 3 Fludd, Robert. *Utriusque cosmi maioris scilicet et minoris (...) historia*, tomus II (1619), tractatus I, sectio I, liber X, *De triplici animae in corpore visione*.

Fig. 4 Edwards, Trystan. *Style and Composition in Architecture* (1926). London: John Tiranti Ltd., 1945, 118–9.

Beatrix Emo, Christoph Hölscher

Fig. 1 Image after Dalton, Ruth Conroy, and Christoph Hölscher. *Take One Building. Interdisciplinary Research Perspectives of the Seattle Central Library*. Abingdon, Oxon: Routledge, 2017.

Peter Holgate

Fig. 1 © Injeong Jo and Sarah Witham Bednarz

Detlef Schulz

Fig. 1 Ostwalds Klassiker der exakten Wissenschaften, *Nr. 235. Euklid: Die Elemente 1. Teil: Buch I–III*. Translated from Greek and edited by Clemens Thaer, Leipzig: Verlag Wilhelm Engelmann, 1933.

Fig. 2 Vitruvio. *I dieci libri di architettura di M. Vitruvio*, tradutti et commentati da Monsignor Barbaro. In Vinegia: per Francesco Marcolini, 1556. © ETH library Zurich, Rar 6731, https://doi.org/10.3931/e-rara-26800/ Public Domain Mark

Fig. 3 Rowe, Colin. *The Mathematics of the Ideal Villa and Other Essays*. Cambridge, Massachusetts and London: MIT Press, 1976.

Fig. 4 Bettagno, Alessandro. *Piranesi*. Vicenza: Neri Pozza Editore, 1978.

Dieter Dietz, Lucía Jalón Oyarzun, Julien Lafontaine Carboni, Teresa Cheung

Fig. 1–4 © Dieter Dietz, Alice, EPFL

Andri Gerber, Michal Berkowitz

Fig. 1 Peters, Michael, Bruno Laeng, Kerry Latham, Marla Jackson, Raghad Zaiyouna, and Chris Richardson. "A Redrawn Vandenberg & Kuse Mental Rotations Test: Different Versions and Factors that affect Performance." In *Brain and Cognition*, 28, 1995. Courtesy of Michael Peter.

Fig. 2 CEEB, *Special Aptitude Test in Spatial Relations*, USA, 1939.

Fig. 3 Kozhevnikov, Maria, and Mary Hegarty. "A dissociation between object manipulation spatial ability and spatial orientation ability." In *Memory & Cognition*. 29 (5), 2001, 745–756. Hegarty, M., and D. Waller. "A dissociation between mental rotation and perspective-taking spatial abilities." In *Intelligence*, *32*(2), 2004, 175–191.

Fig. 4–9 © Michal Berkowitz, Andri Gerber

Cornelie Leopold

Fig. 1–4 © Cornelie Leopold

David Uttal

Fig. 1 I. Resnick, and T. F. Shipley. "Breaking new ground in the mind: an initial study of mental brittle transformation and mental rigid rotation in science experts." In *Cognitive processing, 14* (2), 2013, 143–152. Courtesy Thomas Shipley

Thomas F. Shipley, Noah H. Shipley

Fig. 1–2 © Thomas F. Shipley

Fig. 3 © Jungyoon Kim ©Su-Yeon Angela Choi (MLA 2019 Harvard GSD)

Andri Gerber

Fig. 1–4 © Andri Gerber